SUCCESSFUL POLICE RISK MANAGEMENT

A Guide for Police Executives, Risk Managers, Local Officials, and Defense Attorneys

G. PATRICK GALLAGHER
PRESIDENT, GALLAGHER-WESTFALL GROUP

Copyright © 2014 G. Patrick Gallagher.

All rights reserved. No part of this book may be reproduced, stored, or transmitted by any means—whether auditory, graphic, mechanical, or electronic—without written permission of both publisher and author, except in the case of brief excerpts used in critical articles and reviews. Unauthorized reproduction of any part of this work is illegal and is punishable by law.

ISBN: 978-1-4834-1779-0 (sc)
ISBN: 978-1-4834-1778-3 (e)

Because of the dynamic nature of the Internet, any web addresses or links contained in this book may have changed since publication and may no longer be valid. The views expressed in this work are solely those of the author and do not necessarily reflect the views of the publisher, and the publisher hereby disclaims any responsibility for them.

Any people depicted in stock imagery provided by Thinkstock are models, and such images are being used for illustrative purposes only.
Certain stock imagery © Thinkstock.

Lulu Publishing Services rev. date: 9/11/2014

Dedicated to Mary, who has been by my side for these thirty-four years, who has encouraged and supported me and worked with me, and with whom I share so much happiness

With gratitude for all those who have spent many years
sharing with me innovative ideas and insights for the police
profession and whose dedication to it is unquestioned:

-Bill Westfall for his commitment to police leadership,
-Lou Reiter who speaks so authoritatively on police practices,
-Dr. Jim Ginger whose quality work as a federal
monitor has redirected police agencies,
Pete Sarna, the analyst of police critical incidents par excellence,
Jack Ryan, J.D. the clearest voice of a police legal counsel,
Ron Neubauer for his outstanding example as
chief and of course as a U.S. Marine,
Dave Flaherty, the most eager student of police risk management,
Frank Rodgers whose support for police accreditation
has done so much for New Jersey law enforcement,
Cappy Gagnon for the most incisive insights on policing.

My thanks to Stephanie Olexa, Ph.D. for advice and
assistance in getting this project completed

TABLE OF CONTENTS

Foreword xi
Preface xiii

Chapter 1:
   WHY RISK MANAGEMENT? 1
Chapter 2:
   WHAT'S THIS LIABILITY STUFF? 16
Chapter 3:
   THE OPPOSITION'S GAME PLAN 28
Chapter 4:
   HANDLING POLICE PERFORMANCE DATA 41
Chapter 5:
   PLACING THE EMPHASIS: THE HIGH RISK/
   CRITICAL TASKS 52
Chapter 6:
   SUCCESSFUL PERFORMANCE IN THE HIGH
   RISK/CRITICAL TASKS 64
Chapter 7:
   THE MEANING OF AN OATH 76
Chapter 8:
   SUPERVISION: QUALITY CONTROL FOR
   PERFORMANCE.. 82
Chapter 9:
   VIEWING THE POLICE FROM THE OTHER SIDE 91
Chapter 10:
   PROFESSIONAL STANDARDS AND THE
   DYNAMICS OF POLICIES 97

Chapter 11:
    SIX-LAYERED LIABILITY PROTECTION SYSTEM............116
Chapter 12:
    CASE STUDY: APPLYING THE SIX LAYERS (SLLIPS)........131
Chapter 13:
    STEPS TO TAKE BEFORE AND AFTER LITIGATION.....136
Chapter 14:
    OUR ALLIES: THE INSURANCE AND RISK
    MANAGEMENT POOLS 142
Chapter 15:
    MOVING FORWARD: SUGGESTIONS FOR THE
    ROAD AHEAD 163

Appendix A
    A RESPONSE TO CHAPTER 9, "VIEWING POLICE
    PERFORMANCE FROM THE OTHER SIDE".......................171
Appendix B
    GALLAGHER'S RISK MANAGEMENT PRINCIPLES 195
About the Author 207
Training Available 209

FOREWORD

Pat Gallagher wrote this book for risk managers and any other officials responsible for dealing with police liability oversight. This book should be in the library of every police practitioner, every risk manager, who wants to resist the test of a plaintiff's attack.

While many police practitioners of my generation resented the Monell decision and a number of others as an intrusion into an already complex field, Pat Gallagher realized that the pressure of liability would be the catalyst toward change. With his Six Layers of Liability Protection he created a pro-active process to simplify and manage the complexity of dealing successfully with the problem of liability.

Some day when the police profession reflects it will realize how much Pat Gallagher pioneered police liability management. Thoughtful, Socratic, unselfish and always the mentor and teacher, Pat Gallagher has now written the book to assist police from officer, to supervisor, to chief; to help risk managers and local officials to better understand their critical roles in turning the tide. This is a book full of wise insights and thirty years of thought and practice that will not be duplicated by any other author any time soon, if at all.

Bill Westfall
Gallagher-Westfall Group

PREFACE

Admittedly while so many aspects of police services have been assiduously studied and researched for years, the topic of police risk management has only recently started to garner some attention. Regrettably not enough at the current time to effect a great change or have much of an influence on the delivery of those police services through policy development, more focused and improved training, and most importantly the careful supervision of all police activities. The profession unlike successful businesses does not deal with the analysis of performance data to the point where it culminates in thoughtful changes and overall improvement in every aspect of the tasks which officers are involved in on a daily basis.

Is the profession dealing any more astutely with the problem of liability in the last decade? In the last five years? The judgment remains constant for it seems that there are more exposures, more tasks that generate concern, more lawsuits filed, larger settlements and judgments against police, and legal decisions with complex wordings that further restrict or force modification on our officers.

The liability landscape is populated with more attorneys scrutinizing police actions, and signing up clients who have been involved with police. Alleged negligence or a variety of constitutional violations are asserted. At that point police organizations are required to divert a sizable part of their resources to produce documents, to make the named officers available for depositions and trials, and to shoulder the stress of a prolonged chapter in the litigational history of one department.

Even with more research and study, what is lacking as I see it, is the perception as to where to initiate our defensive mode and what process can assuredly be implemented in the administrative and operational world of policing to produce positive results.

I hold that the insight needed is to concentrate on the quality of preparing for performance, carrying it out, and then reviewing it with the greatest scrutiny. Poor performance is the raw material so essential to the plaintiffs' objectives. It is what feeds the liability machine. Deny them performance that is questionable, or that is short of professional standards and we will accrue the greatest results. Fail to do this and the problem will always be with us.

I propose that with a single-minded focus on performance and with the application of the Six Layers of Liability Protection System (S.L.L.I.P.S.) where our efforts maximize the quality of each layer that results can be guaranteed. This will allow the profession to deal with liability in a more proactive manner, rather than relying so heavily on a good defense.

We cannot continue to bemoan the burden of liability and its concomitant distraction from the delivery of services unless we commit ourselves to a process that assuredly will stem the tide in our favor. Will it be easy? There is no facile solution, but these two objectives: focus on performance and implementation of the S.L.L.I.P.S. process over time will lighten the burden.

CHAPTER 1
WHY RISK MANAGEMENT?

"You can only beat or manage a system that you understand. Chiefs, sheriffs, supervisors and officers can beat any system that they understand."
                                            -Gallagher's Principles #1

"Every discussion of duty has two parts. One part deals with the question of the supreme good. The other deals with the rules that should guide us in ordering our lives."
                                            -Cicero

Alice meets the Cheshire cat at a fork in the road and asks: "Which road should I take?'"
The Cheshire cat asks: "Where are you going?"
Alice answered: "I don't know."
The Cheshire cat says: "That's easy. Either road will take you there!"
                            -Lewis Carroll in <u>Alice in Wonderland</u>

There once was a physics professor who posed this problem during a test: "How do you find the height of a building using a barometer?" One student pondered this question for a while and then wrote down: "Go to the top of the building, tie a string to the barometer, and lower the string over the side of the building until it hits the ground. Then measure the length of the string."

The student received a zero as his grade for this bit of casuistry. He protested vociferously and eventually the professor -battered by the student's complaints- agreed to a retest. The retest needed to be monitored by a colleague of the professor and needed to demonstrate the student's knowledge of physics.

As the seconds clicked away the student -seemingly befuddled by the problem- did not begin until the monitor asked him if he were stumped. "No," said the student, "there are just so many solutions I can't decide which to submit," but quickly scribbled down this answer: "Take the barometer and go to the top of the building and then drop it over the side, timing the barometer's fall with a stopwatch. Using the formula of $D=1/2gt^2$ or distance equals one-half the speed of gravity multiplied by the square of the time in seconds, and *Voila!* you have the height of the building." His original professor gave him an almost perfect grade.

Puzzled, the monitor followed the student and asked this question of him: "You said there were so many other solutions. What were they?" The student replied: "You can go into the staircase and applying the barometer against the wall, find out the height of the building in barometer lengths. Or you could go out on a sunny day, set up the barometer, measure its height and that of its shadow, and then measure the length of the building's shadow. Use a simple proportion and you have the height of the building. Another method is to go to the top of the building and get the barometric pressure there and at ground level and theoretically you have the height of the building." That professor was impressed.

"Finally," said the student, "you can go down to the basement of the building and knock on the building manager's door, and say to him, 'Sir, I have here a fine barometer, and if you tell me the height of the building, I will give you the barometer.'"

As illustrated in the professor/student exchange, we have to look for the simplest approach. The physics professor was fixated on one solution. In fact, although the student's solution was perfectly correct, showing a knowledge of physics, one employing a stopwatch, the professor could only begrudgingly grant close to a perfect score. The student "thinking outside of the box" came up with several solutions, but chose the easiest.

The lesson? If liability is the universal problem it is purported to be, look to the easiest and most effective answers to the problem. Does the police profession have a solid plan for combatting liability? If not, why not?

How we arrived here

In the last quarter of a century law enforcement has been subjected to a veritable onslaught of lawsuits, which has resulted in continuous litigation. This litigation has depleted our resources, and our corporate energies, distracted us from the primary concerns of "protecting and serving," eroded the public's support, and possibly tarnished our image with the public.

Yet our officers have worked extremely diligently to maintain levels of service, and police executives have grappled with the constant increases in calls-for-service, in demands for responses to a wider variety of demanding tasks, and the possibilities of renewed threats from a range of dangerous sources.

What do we do as a profession? Stand and absorb the repeated blows? Or be reminded of Shakespeare's conflicted Hamlet when he asks:

> "To be or not to be. That is the question:
> Whether 'tis nobler in the mind to suffer
> The slings and arrows of outrageous fortune,
> Or to take arms against a sea of troubles
> And by opposing, end them?"

I sense that there is this same quandary out there, that no one wants to endure "the slings and arrows of outrageous fortune" which seem to go so heavily against us. Admittedly, however, the clear vision and plan are lacking, not totally formed, or for the most part, not operational. All the while there are factors that tell us in no uncertain terms that the opposition is strengthened by the omnipresent video evidence that alleges abuses and violations. Do the "Cops" video series of television always show officers at their best, observing all the constitutional requirements and never stepping over the line and acting contrary to professional standards?

We can do better than the present response to liability.

The obvious questions

Some questions are in order:

1. After our experience of the last twenty-five years, we might have hoped we would have seen liability in our rearview mirror. But have we come any closer to taming the liability problem? Are plaintiffs' attorneys getting frustrated with no returns from lawsuits launched against police?
2. Can we say that we are smarter in dealing with the particular issues and tasks that apparently generate so much litigation?
3. Are we learning through all of our individual and corporate experiences (some very expensive ones) how to work smarter?
4. From all our corporate and individual experiences, have we learned better how to be on the winning side more frequently when we are sued?
5. Have we reached the point of accepting the costs of litigation, the settlements and adverse judgments as the cost of doing business? Have we become somewhat comfortable with a certain degree of litigation?
6. Most importantly have we figured out the means of depriving plaintiffs' attorneys of the raw material that keeps them in business?

Candidly, what's our response?

If we base our judgment on winning cases in court, do we win more often because we have better defense counsels? Or because we did everything right? The ultimate goal should not be winning in court, although it is acceptable. The ultimate goal to stem the attacks is to deny the plaintiffs' attorneys the very resource that keeps them in business. How do you help them go out of business or into another line of legal involvement?

The quality of police performance is what keeps the attorneys in business. That is the one element that encourages them to stay in business. If the quality of performance is poor or below standards they can hope to thrive in their line of work. Our challenge is to staunch the flow of raw material to them: the incidents of police activity. The initiation of possible liability starts with the action of officers on the street. <u>Therein lies the secret to reducing</u>

liability. It depends on how we deal with it. The struggle should be won in the streets. But our efforts there must be buttressed before, during and after that action, by increasing attention to the systemic improvement in the quality of that action.

John Foster Dulles has said: "The mark of a successful organization is not whether or not it has problems, but whether it has the same problems year after year." We might pose the same question: How long has this problem, (that is liability), been of this magnitude? How long has it been with us? To what extent are we as a profession responsible for the long term existence and growth of the problem? What positive steps are we taking to reduce this problem?

How successful are we in reducing liability?

Responding to that question, are our organizations successful? In some respects, to say "no" might be too harsh a judgment, since we are more successful, and more competent at a lot of functions. But could we be even better? Do we maintain a type of candid discontent in the face of the highest achievement? I think anyone would give a resounding nod to that question. That only raises a query: "How do we become more successful at dealing with the liability problem, with limiting its inroads, and decreasing our losses?"

Police are very competitive; they don't like losing. They certainly do not feel good at the repeated notoriety they receive from the latest mega-million dollar settlement or judgment against them. With the profusion of dashcam videos can we as police professionals be totally objective enough to state officers' performances are always up to our highest standards?

While it is true police don't like losing, they overlook that the cost of losing is borne by others. So in one sense while somewhat distanced from that aspect of the loss as the insurance companies and the risk management pools pay out, they might fail to realize the taint that all police departments, and all police suffer from any loss. There must be a crystallizing moment when this no longer happens with the frequency that it occurs today. Police must realize that winning is more than getting a favorable verdict; rather that it is an affirmation that their conduct and their administrative efforts were totally vindicated through the litigation process. Better still is the win on a daily basis when there is absolutely no incident that could ever be questioned as to its adherence to professional standards, regardless of whether or not someone wants to expend their energies in launching a suit.

That's what I want to speak to, for I know there are certain steps, selected and proven processes that if implemented comprehensively and accompanied by the required compliance, that will shrink the problem. That's a guarantee!

How's this for a vision?

Suppose you had a vision of all the plaintiffs' attorneys and you found them all sleeping on park benches. What would that mean? What's its significance? It would be perfectly clear they are out of business. They are out of business as far as police liability goes because we have deprived them of the raw material essential to their livelihood. That material is police performance, which the attorneys consider questionable, below professional standards, and in violation of a person's constitutional rights. These elements finally generate a complaint, a claim and eventually a lawsuit. While we may like the vision, the question remains: How do we achieve it? What do we have to do? Are we willing to do what it takes?

Are we paying too much?

One of Gallagher's Principles is: "If you don't mind paying the price of doing business the way you are, then change nothing. If you don't want to pay that price, then in some ways you have to change the way you do business." In the May 2014 issue of **Police Chief** in the article "Managing Change: A Success Story in a Culture Resistant to Change," writers Doug LePard and Michelle Davey comment: "A truism in policing is that the only thing cops hate more than change is the way things are."

If an organization or a profession over time gets too comfortable, gets too accustomed to doing things one way, if it gets too myopic and does not discern what the losses actually are or the price it is paying, it becomes a more daunting task to change for the better. It's that simple. If we measure success or lack of it by the increase or decrease in the number of suits, or by the amount paid out in settlements or judgments, or by the millions expended in expenses even if we win, then we can't say we are truly successful.

If settlements, judgments and their attendant expenses are merely acceptable as the costs of doing business, those costs are only going to accelerate as more plaintiffs' attorneys decide to make their fortunes from our police organizations. The only alternative to that fate is a concerted effort at practical risk management methods that will create a shift in the balance, will reduce the costs and take the tremendous burden off the shoulders of the police and our communities. However, this will only occur if we commit ourselves to certain steps, the performance of all police tasks in conformity with constitutional requirements, state statutes, and departmental policies and training. That's it!

Keeping pace with the plaintiff's bar

The plaintiff's bar is getting smarter, learning new methods to launch a suit against us. They are incentivized as never before to win and win big. It has been said: "A smart person learns from his own mistakes. An intelligent person learns from the mistakes of others." What do you call a person who learns from neither?

Go back to the expression "the way we do business," which is really our performance. Have you ever thought about this liability process and the means of reducing its burden in this manner? When addressing the problem, police professionals constantly think in terms of better policies, more training, tighter supervision, and necessary corrective action. As important as these are, they are only inputs into the system, carrying our hopes that they will change the dynamic. We must think not exclusively in terms of inputs, but focus on the one critical, essential output. That is <u>performance</u>.

We need to see that with laser-like exactitude, plaintiffs' attorneys' focus on performance. What attracts them to police activity is the manner in which police perform their range of activities. As they focus on performance, they have learned that certain types of performance- from <u>their</u> perspective - are more productive to achieve their ends.

From our side, our perspective must be to thwart them at the point where they are most likely to be looking, which is, again, performance. Policy, training, supervision and corrective action are inputs, purposely improved to do one thing, improve performance. This is the only acceptable result of those efforts.

The only acceptable output of an organization is high level performance

Every complaint, every claim, every lawsuit is a commentary on one thing. It is not policy, training, supervision or discipline, but performance. People file lawsuits because of a dissatisfaction with performance, not with the policies, training or supervision. Those people who eventually become plaintiffs allege our performance fell short of professional standards. The inputs: policy, training, supervision and discipline are inputs whose purpose is to heighten performance. That must be our goal and the only acceptable outcome. Yes, our efforts at improving the inputs will contribute mightily to performance, but it is performance that must be tightly examined, evaluated, and improved.

If plaintiffs' attorneys focus on performance as the requisite resource for them to stay in existence, and if every lawsuit is filed because of dissatisfaction with performance, what is it that must focus on? It is undoubtedly performance. Yes, I am belaboring that point, but it is because I feel we have concentrated on the inputs, felt satisfied, and slacked off on the necessary concentration on performance.

That leads us to Gallagher's Principle 20:

> **"Anything that inhibits high level performance must be decreased or better still eliminated. Anything that helps officers perform better must be increased."**

I am convinced that our efforts at better policies, at accreditation, more training, and better equipment will fall short of achieving the anticipated outcome and desired goal - the decrease or elimination of the pressure of liability. Why? Because while truly beneficial, those factors have to be integrated into a total process that includes not only an identification of the focus of our efforts, i.e. performance, but on a process that considers the strategies of the plaintiff's bar. This strengthens our defenses to make us as invulnerable as possible.

The components of an effective liability reduction program

In subsequent chapters I will lay out the components of this process which if brought together and implemented in one agency can turn the tide against the liability tsunami. It can take this burden of liability off our backs and restore more control over our agencies. Think of it: in light of what might appear to be a lack of control, of alleged performances drastically departing from accepted professional standards, external forces then enter the picture and require specified steps to take place, which force us to change.

Witness the New Jersey State Police after the federal consent decree and the many other jurisdictions that had the federal courts and federal monitors enter their space, requiring compliance to any number of standards. Witness the additional requirements imposed by the New Jersey Attorney General's Office after the A.C.L.U. surveyed New Jersey police departments statewide on the subject of complaint taking. That's just one state. In a recent article in the F.B.I. National Academy Associates by Dr. Jeffrey Phillips, "Measuring Law Enforcement Performance," twenty-six agencies are listed as a starting point for investigations with M.O.U.s and consent decrees emanating from a number of them on the basis of "a pattern of constitutional violations."

Certain changes, combined with a commitment to a complete organization-wide process for diminishing the impact of liability are within our grasp. Our profession should not be forced to take directions from external entities but to achieve the goal we have to make the requisite modifications in our strategic approach to liability management while convincing these outside forces that we can change our organizations as necessary.

We all want progress in every field, and certainly in law enforcement. But many tend to shy away from change. Progress and change go hand in hand. Organizations of every kind, the literature tells us, either achieve a greater and more complete mastery of their operations or become more ineffective with their problems swelling to larger proportions. There is no stasis; there is no equilibrium where the organization remains exactly the same.

As Lou Reiter, retired deputy chief of the L.A.P.D. said: "Organizational change comes about through gentle pressure relentlessly applied." Is it our reality that we have sought change "through massive pressure infrequently applied?" Unquestionably, it is time to accept changes that will make a world of difference when it is coupled with a selection of risk management techniques. More on that later.

Risk management among police

As police executives and managers improve their capabilities to control, improve and lead their departments, there is one glaring deficiency: the absence of emphasis on risk management. Loss control and risk management have long been terms not associated with police departments. Police agencies just didn't spend much time attempting to control losses, to decrease them or to manage risk, in a profession which by the profession's very nature is fraught with risk.

Assuredly police manage risk when it comes to the dangers that officers face; we prepare programs to manage risk when the community's safety is involved. But it is undeniable that policing of necessity does a lot of risk management applied to critical events and to even the more mundane tasks of traffic stops and warrant service. We look for the potential of attack or injury, and we take steps to counter those dangers. Risk management applied to liability requires the application of the same skills and the same attention.

However, when it comes to identifying, assessing and limiting those risks associated with liability there is a form of A.D.D. or "attention deficit disorder" that allows our administrators to overlook, or not pay the necessary attention to risk management. Yet I hold it is a skill and a function that must be integrated into the entire span of management responsibilities.

If risk management concepts drive police performance there will be two solid effects: liability will be decreased and organizational professionalism will be enhanced.

If you search through the literature on police risk management you may be disappointed. It was only in the last decade that there has been a systemic assessment of the apparent absence of risk management from our police agencies.

Risk management in policing has been a neglected topic in police literature. In 2001, Dr. Sam Walker mentioned this topic in **Police Accountability: The Role of Citizen Oversight** and stated that:

> "One of the most notable failures of both police departments and other city officials has been their neglect of modern concepts of risk management and in particular their refusal to examine incidents that result in litigation and seek to correct the underlying problems."

Dr. Walker attributes the high cost of litigation to the:

> "frequent misconduct by officers in the street and civil rights attorneys believing that certain cities are 'easy touches' and readily settle misconduct suits in amounts that make litigation worth the efforts."

Not much has changed in the interim. A slight sense of the extent of the problem might be gained from a daily reading of www.policemisconduct.net which will list nationwide the misconduct and outright criminal activity of police officers and the status of various lawsuits filed against them. Daily the roll call of events can be discouraging for it can serve to taint the selfless, professional dedication of hundreds of thousands of other officers who do their duty and assume their responsibilities.

The settlements of lawsuits are not only driven by defense attorneys sensing that their case is not strong enough but the tendency to push the case as far as possible looking for exposed weaknesses on the plaintiff's side. Finding on the contrary strong evidence that the opposition might prevail, they opt for recommending a settlement.

However, in my personal experience, there have been examples where there was total agreement about the strength of the case, and of the gradual deterioration of the plaintiff's case, when the insurance carrier's worries increased to the point that their people ordered a sizable settlement. The attorneys were never polled and the representatives of the insurance company were never present in court for one session. The insurance company had nothing on which to base its decision to settle, but settle they did which created disappointment to say the least for the defense attorneys and a struck a massive blow to the morale of the involved officers.

In one of the studies in the last couple of years about the place of risk management in policing Dr. Carol Archbold found in her pioneering effort there was not much to study. In conducting a literature search on this topic, she found one book written by this author in 1992 titled: **Risk Management Behind the Blue Curtain: A Primer on Law Enforcement Liability**.

Her article "Managing the Bottom Line: Risk Management in Policing," (**Policing: An International Journal of Police Strategies and Management**, Vol. 28, No. 1, 2005) made efforts to clearly define the topic and to assess to what extent police departments made use of risk management "to control police-related liability." In her nationwide survey she uncovered only 14 out of 354 of the largest departments in the country did just that.

But while a few departments could say that they had some element of risk management with the purpose of controlling liability, it is my observation that the recommendations and findings are not really integrated into the overall management decisions of those agencies.

Dr. Archbold outlines the five steps or phases in risk management germane to either hospital management or policing. In looking at these phases you can readily see how relevant they can be to policing for they are to:

1. identify risks, frequency of exposure to risks, and the severity of losses using data on the history of loss to include past lawsuits, complaints and payouts;
2. explore methods to handle exposure to identified risks reviewing policies and procedures, training and supervision;
3. choose appropriate treatment or response to manage exposure to risks by changing policies, training and/or supervision;
4. implement risk treatment and all changes to policies, procedures and training;
5. continuously evaluate risk treatment.

As she correctly points out the process is not complete in the first four phases but must include an ongoing fifth phase which is alerting the organization to the fine tuning of the process, the need for additional changes in policies and training, or the selection of different supervisory styles. Evaluation, review and revision are key concepts and as such they are never complete.

This important information is not factored into the management of present day police departments, and in my opinion the profession will never substantially cut into the ever increasing losses from liability until we incorporate these steps into our management. This book will speak more to what a department can do in a very concrete manner for all five of those phases.

To reinforce the almost complete absence of affirmative programs resulting from litigation and/or the failure to employ the data emanating from this litigation, Johanna C. Swartz in "Myths and Mechanics of Deterrence: Litigation, Information, and Decision Making," **(U.C.L.A. Law Review, volume 57, September 2009)** surveyed twenty large police departments only to find it was the exceptional department that utilized any of the data from lawsuits constructively to affect police performance.

When suits were filed the names of the officers involved were not forwarded to Internal Affairs for investigation; it was only when the plaintiff filed a formal complaint against the officer, that the departments would investigate. This stance pushed to the extreme was exemplified by a police spokesperson who was asked for comments about a video showing a subject on the ground being beaten and kicked by an officer. Yes, he remarked they would investigate the incident but only if the subject filed a formal complaint.

As befits the largest police organization in the country, the New York Police Department's officers get sued frequently. The city has paid out a billion dollars in the last decade according to a **New York Daily News** investigative team who reviewed the 9570 suits filed in 2012 to find the officers who had the most lawsuits filed against them. The February 16, 2014 **Daily News** article indicated there were 12 officers sued more than 17 times between 2006 and 2013. It appeared until recently that the New York Police Department was not tracking on lawsuits or the officers involved until the data was pried loose from the admittedly incomplete records by a Freedom of Information Act request by the **Daily News**.

The **Daily News** article identified one officer who averaged about 4 lawsuits at year for a total of 28 suits during that seven year span. The New York Police Department paid out $884,004 in settlements for what were seen mainly as problems with arrests. The officer according to the article augmented his base salary of $87,278 with $38,000 in overtime in 2013 and ranked in the

99th percentile for overtime income in the department. (In April of 2014, the **Daily News** in a follow-up article wrote that this officer was removed from his street assignment and stationed inside.)

The question could be raised that you do not need a computer program to identify and take some action in a situation like this. Where were his supervisors? What were they doing as on average a new suit was filed against him every three months? Was there nothing in his actions, or his reports that led supervisors to question his performance? Or were those supervisors focused exclusively on the officer's "productivity" with little scrutiny on his methodology in those arrests?

Another point: since most of the lawsuits were associated with problems with arrests, you would think that some supervisor would see a pattern, would take the officer aside for some counseling, would assign him to additional training, or would initiate a more careful review of all of his arrests. This pattern of conduct generated no known additional scrutiny or remediation.

Going back to the 1990s repeated requests from the former city controller for the NYPD to tabulate data on lawsuits linking them with the involved officers were not honored, until the last six months or so when the controller's office formed Claimstat. In the waning days of Commissioner Kelly's administration he originated a risk assessment unit. Commissioner Bratton according to the article is looking at ways to improve both the monitoring program and the risk assessment unit to identify potential problem officers.

On August 6, 2014 the new head of the Civilian Complaint Review Board in New York announced the formation of what is tentatively called "Cop-stat" to serve as an early warning system and to amalgamate all complaints so that department brass might be "forewarned about the things that are developing or percolating up," as stated by board chair Richard Emery. Another expressed purpose of this program is to access the "trove of information that tells us what is going on in police community relations that we have not tapped" in the past.

Historically when the principal actors on the liability stage are listed: the citizens, the courts, the media, the plaintiffs' bar and of course the police, it must be recognized that nothing will change in the attitudes and commitments of any of them. The only one group that police can influence with an eye to decreasing the burden of liability is the profession itself. To change the outcome police must deliver services at a higher, more liability-proof level.

We cannot continue to bemoan the problem; the profession is not being victimized; steps have to be taken to put together a process which if followed will yield more than just promising results. It will basically guarantee the level of performance will rise while lawsuits and the onerous burden of litigation will drop off precipitously.

Police executives are too far removed from the lawsuit continuum. They certainly have enough concerns and worries, but in neglecting to factor in an ongoing involvement in more of the details of the litigation, they are missing an opportunity to truly perfect their managerial skills that would come through integrating risk management principles into the corpus of their job responsibilities.

CHAPTER 2

WHAT'S THIS LIABILITY STUFF?

"Police management is driven more by the constraints of the job, rather than the goals of the job."
                -James Q. Wilson and George Kelling

"No law book, no lawyer, no judge can really tell the police officer on the beat how to exercise this discretion perfectly in every one of the thousands of different situations that can arise in the hour-to-hour work of the police officer. Yet we must recognize that we need not choose between no guidelines at all and perfect guidelines. There must be some guidance by way of basic concepts that will assist the officers in these circumstances."
                -Chief Justice Warren Burger

An awful lot can be said about liability as it relates to police officers and police operations. I would like to distill it down to some basic and simple definitions. For a more complete and expanded discussion of the topic you can pick up the popular **Critical Issues in Police Civil Liability** by Victor E. Kappler, now in its fourth edition, a testament to its popularity.

Tracking on the Wilson and Kelling quote, civil liability does something to focus the attention of police management to the extent that it increasingly colors management decisions and even that of the officers in the street. I would claim that the attention must be given not so much to the restraints but to the methods that will lessen the impact it has on our decision making and the manner in which we do business.

Acknowledging that the problem of liability does not make our jobs easier, we must realize how much the focus on the problem of liability detracts from our ability to perform our job and all of our responsibilities at a peak performance level. Liability is the unconscious presence looking over our shoulders; it is the force that has officers hesitate at times to take action; it is the fear of being stigmatized with a lawsuit filing when police have truly done their very best.

The sources of lawsuits

Providing police services is inherently risky; we have to control those risks. As someone has facetiously remarked: "We could cut down on lawsuits if we could get an unlisted phone for our department." Lawsuits are the progeny of complaints when people are dissatisfied with some form of the services provided to them by police. Real or imagined, the complaint once filed might lead to a claim against the police department, and ultimately to the filing of a lawsuit.

In some cases there is no complaint, no claim. An incident takes place, and hordes of attorneys become interested in representing the victim who might never have thought of initiating any action against the officer or the city. It has been determined that some plaintiffs' attorneys don't want their clients to file a complaint. Rather, they rely on the lawsuit to place all the details of the case before the court.

Suits originate from claims of negligence and from claims of constitutional violations usually with the former filed in state courts and with the latter in federal courts.

Negligence

In attempting to distill the process I will state at risk of oversimplifying that negligence suits come from complaints about inadequate police services, services short of standards. There was something that the officers did, that they should not have done; or they should not have done it in the manner which they did; or finally they should not have done anything at all. That failure caused some injury or loss.

The classic manner to explain the concept of negligence suits describes what I call the "four pillars" principle. Picture a bridge with four sets of pillars supporting it. The four pillars are as follows:

1. a **duty** owed according to a standard of care;
2. a **failure** to perform that duty according to the standard of care;
3. an **injury** or **loss;**
4. a causal **connection** between the **failure** to perform according to the standard of care and the **injury** or **loss**.

In this bridge analogy, the plaintiff's attorney has to push his case across the four pillars, across the bridge. He has to prove and connect all four points to make the case for negligence. The test applied which determines the expectations of the court and the plaintiff is "reasonableness."

Witness the following instructions by a judge to a jury in a negligence case:

> "Failure to take **reasonable** care which a **reasonably** careful person would use under like circumstances, doing something a **reasonably** careful person would not do, or failing to do something a **reasonably** careful person would do."

So whether it is driving a patrol car, answering a call, or transporting a person the test of reasonableness is applied. Professional police standards give us the benchmarks for what is reasonable, what is to be expected of an officer handling this task, or performing this assignment. These standards are articulated in police policies, directives, rules and regulations and of course in training.

But there is no mystery to it, avoiding negligence suits comes down to being properly trained in how to do tasks and then to doing it just that way. This brings me to one of Gallagher's Principles # 26:

> **"There is nothing you should do to manage liability that you should not already be doing as a good leader, a good manager, a good supervisor, and a good officer."**

What is it that police do? In developing Job Task Analyses for police there are almost 700 discrete tasks which officers have to perform. Most are probably never implicated when it comes to a liability suit. A few have a much higher profile and a lot more litigation activity. But for any professional, be this person a pilot, doctor, engineer, or a lawyer, professional standards of care guide them in every task they perform. Police officers as professionals are under the same obligation to observe and follow closely the standards of care.

Supervisory negligence

Supervisors are those persons charged with overseeing the manner in which others, their subordinates, perform their work. Supervisors have additional responsibilities. They are tasked with making sure that others carry out their assignments with adherence to the professional standards of care. They also have to guarantee that within their scope of responsibility if someone is markedly departing from the standards of care, they should take notice, correct the officer, provide remediation through retraining or counseling, or even possibly discipline to bring them into line. Finally if their subordinates are not coming up the standard in their actions they must not participate alongside them. Negligence for supervisors can be direct or indirect.

Direct supervisory negligence

There are four ways that a supervisor could be directly negligent. I use the acronym "PARD" to remember this.

P articipates if the supervisor participates in the action which is opposed to professional standards;
A uthorizes if the supervisor in effect tells the subordinates to go ahead and do the particular action, or how to do it;
R atifies if once the action is performed the supervisor says that it is acceptable, that he/she signs off on it;
D irects if the supervisor orders officers to take some action, or tells them not to do something that they should have done.

There are occasions when supervisors sign off on officers' incident reports either without reading them critically or reading them and knowing full well what really took place out on the street. One supervisor in a busy sector actually responded to my question about processing the officers' reports by saying: "I just sign them. You don't expect me to read all of them, do you?"

My response was: "I certainly do, because by that signature you are tying yourself to whatever the officer did." Of course, if supervisors universally do not read all reports closely and then occasionally reject some, or don't ask some follow-up questions, they are associating themselves with that action.

Indirect supervisory negligence

Direct supervisory negligence has the supervisor closely involved either in the incident, or just before it, or in following it up. Indirect supervisory negligence on the other hand exists when the action of the supervisor is at once removed in time (possibly years) and place from the location and the date of the incident.

But despite the distance, the supervisors by their actions are considered responsible for the burden is "imposed on one who is without fault in the violation, simply because of a particular relationship of responsibility borne toward the person actually performing the act." The reasoning is that the negligence would not have occurred if the supervisor by some previous involvement had not been negligent. The negligence of the supervisor allows the actor, the one performing the actual negligence to be in a position to do the act. Indirect supervisory negligence does not happen in a vacuum; it is lodged against supervisors when their subordinates perform an act giving rise to the lawsuit.

We might sum up the eight generally accepted forms of indirect supervisory negligence as follows by the acronym of **ART'S DEAD**:

A ppointment:- in 12/13/ the LASO admitted appointing 80 officers from a disbanded agency to the LASO. Some had criminal convictions; some had not been trained. They could not be fired so they had to be given selected assignments.
R etention: - retaining an officer whose performance record clearly indicates that he/she abuses authority, consistently uses excessive force, or had been found to steal from arrested subjects.
T raining: - given the tasks the officer has to perform failing to train that officer adequately. The **Canton** case in the late 1980s is a perfect example of a manager tasked with determining whether or not a person would get medical attention, but having no training for

this task. Also one agency had its recruits study the laws of arrest through home study, and then they made some highly questionable arrests.

- **S upervision:** - failing to observe officers' performance, to correct improper performance, to evaluate performance and to recommend remedial or corrective action
- **D irection:** - failing to articulate to personnel clearly how duties are to be performed
- **E ntrustment:** - giving officers equipment for which they have not been adequately trained. A major city never checked to see if academy graduates had a driver's license and assigned them to patrol units. In case of an injury to a pedestrian in the course of a pursuit, the supervisor (chief) would be hard put to make any defense.
- **A ssignment:** - assigning an officer to a position or duty that he/she is incapable of performing if a person is injured as a result, say a bomb sweep where an untrained officer misses the bomb and someone is injured.
- **D iscipline:** - failure to consistently take any action in the face of serious misconduct or illegal activity or a pattern of not investigating adequately and finding all complaints unsubstantiated.

In 2013 in Catalonia, Spain a police officer trying to arrest two martial artists for extortion got the approval of his supervisor to use a stun grenade when the artists wouldn't leave the car. He tossed the grenade into one man's lap, causing the man to lose one testicle, The other became damaged, and subsequently the man became infertile. The judge sentenced the officer to jail, said it was gross negligence, and told him to pay the man $230,000. In our terminology this could possibly be a trifecta, that is: negligent training, entrustment and supervision.

The charges associated with indirect supervisory negligence are always attached to the details and circumstances of the incident itself. Supervisory negligence in its various forms does not stand alone. While the burden of proof is the same, the preponderance of the evidence, it is a lot more difficult for plaintiffs' attorneys to prove this negligence in its various forms. However that does not deter them from including it in most complaints. Moreover, in my experience this padding of the complaint with these additional charges does not go too far. The opposition makes little progress in proving these allegations and by the end of discovery they are frequently dismissed.

But when the list of possibilities of indirect supervisory negligence are examined, every example is a solid management and supervisory responsibility. Supervisors and managers exist to do those very functions; to fail at doing them properly according to professional standards is to fail at management and supervision. Gallagher's Principles #15 states: "There is a direct correlation between good management and quality supervision and liability management."

Constitutional violations

At the beginning of this chapter I said lawsuits come from two sources: negligence and constitutional violations. Now we will look at the latter source, where it is alleged and how a subject's constitutional rights are violated.

The Big Five in the wake of the Civil Rights Act of 1871

They are:

>**Monroe v. Pape,** (1965)
>**Monell v. the New York Department of Social Services** (1978)
>**Garner v. Tennessee** (1985)
>**Canton v. Harris** (1988)
>**Graham v. Connor** (1989)

After the Civil War it was found that the right to vote and own property was being restricted especially in the southern states. Congress immediately passed the Civil Rights Act, also called the Ku Klux Klan Act. Codified as 42 USC, section 1983 it warned officials that they were liable if they acted under color of law, and subjected a person to a deprivation of the rights that were secured by the constitution or other laws.

We could say that the mind of the congress was focused on voting and owning property. The modicum of activity under this act dealt with these two violations. Police liability? It was totally quiescent until the mid-1960s when some lawyers thought they could file cases under this act for police actions such as alleged false arrest, illegal searches and excessive force after the lawyers asked, "Weren't the officers' actions constitutional violations? Weren't they public officials even though they were not mayors or city council persons?"

Welcome to the age of police litigation! As attorneys will do they pushed out the limits of the law, probing and testing for its outer reaches. Where **Monroe** found police officers guilty of constitutional violations for false arrest, illegal searches and excessive force, their administrators and the departments themselves were immune for they were not "persons" as defined by the U.S. Supreme Court decision. One could not sue an administrator or a department; **Monroe** in effect accorded them immunity.

Not to worry! In **Monell** twelve years later, the Supreme Court decreed that if the department and its executives by their policies were directly instrumental in causing the violations actually committed by their officers, then the department and the executive could be found guilty. This decision was the signal for plaintiffs' attorneys to go after the "deep pocket" for much larger damages.

Garner limited the use of deadly force by police to serious felonies where the officer had been threatened or the officer has probable cause to believe the subject had committed a crime involving the infliction or threatened infliction of serious physical harm.

Canton, previously alluded to, deals with the necessity of training officers in the light of the tasks assigned to them. Nothing radical here; if an officer is going to perform a task then the executive cannot be "deliberatively indifferent" to the adequate training necessary to perform the task correctly without denying some constitutional rights.

Finally, **Graham** mandated that the officers' actions in using force must be governed by the "objectively reasonableness" principle in the light of the totality of the circumstances in which the officer finds himself but with no consideration of underlying intention. Few decisions have had as much impact on police training, police policy, and ultimately supervision as this one.

The progeny of these cases is threaded through all of the many decisions handed down by the federal courts and their appellate levels. It should go without saying that our officers should be thoroughly well-versed in these cases especially **Graham** for all of its influence on any possible use of force.

Having said this, how do we explain that even in the last few years, over two decades in the aftermath of **Graham** I have come across training materials that have **Johnson v. Glick** as the standard indicating the serious lack of the basic care and concern for updating critical legal requirements. **Johnson** was replaced by **Graham** substituting objective reasonableness for **Johnson**'s subjective reasonableness. The standard became what would the reasonably well trained officer do in this situation. What force would he/she employ?

Smart vs. wise

Again, someone has said:

> "There is a difference between being smart and wise. Smart ones learn from their own experience. Wise ones learn from the experience of others."

With the welter of lawsuits in every state and federal court, and in the decisions of the U.S. Supreme Court the police profession certainly has enough indications of the legal expectations for the conduct of its officers. Every department right down to the local level has seen the outcomes of numerous lawsuits possibly to its own organization or to its neighbors.

From every one of those decisions and judgments, there are the lessons to be drawn, lessons which tell us in no uncertain terms what we must do. It flows undoubtedly from there, that policies have to be changed, training upgraded, and supervisory and management oversight has to be improved.

If you're smart and you learn from your own experience, and if, better still, you are wise and you learn from the experience of others, what would characterize those who learn from neither? What about those who blithely go on their way and operate their agencies paying little if any attention to the legal landscape?

Possible reasons

I think there are three reasons why the profession does not learn enough from our pyrrhic losses, or our many "successes" in the legal arena.

1. What does victory or success mean?

I think we look to the number of victories or successes and start to feel overconfident. Yes, we win outright when the case goes to court and our officers have done the right thing in the right way at the right time, and we can prove this. Yes, we win often if that means avoiding a catastrophic judgment. Sometimes we can consider it a win when we settle to avoid allowing a jury to make its decision. Or we settle in a very high percentage of cases even before it goes to court.

As far as the legal strategy is concerned, there is no denying that there might be sound reasons for settlement short of a judgment since it might be for a figure less than we project the jury might go for. In federal courts, abbreviating the legal proceedings could drastically decrease the legal fees for a protracted court conflict. Have we really won when our officers are under the stress of seeing their names on a filed suit for years? Have we won when they have to prepare for depositions and then sit there to be deposed? Have we won when we settle for the lesser amount strictly as a business decision?

2. Lack of feedback

Seldom do the defense attorneys provide solid feedback on all aspects of the case to the insurance/risk management pool, or the individual department. By comprehensive feedback, I mean candid analysis of the defense case, the materials submitted, the possible shortcomings of the plaintiff's representatives. Feedback to include a series of recommendations that would place the department in a much stronger basis.

3. Lack of respect for our opponents

That's not to say we want to necessarily make friends and share a drink with those who vigorously represent the plaintiff's cause. But let's respect their experience and ability to get a particularly nasty job accomplished.

Let's face it, many plaintiffs' attorneys know the intricacies of the legal process and when presented with our documents through discovery they can easily capitalize on them, by highlighting the inadequacies in policies, training, supervision, corrective action, and finally the reports and depositions of our personnel. How often do the officers and supervisors in depositions present the strongest statement of the proper performance for our side?

From my experience working almost exclusively with defense cases, I am hard pressed to defend these shortcomings. Yes, the positive elements can be voiced in reports, depositions and testimony. (Particularly with training documents which because of my background in training and educational methodologies, I can see more of the inadequacies.) I know that it is only with time that the plaintiffs' attorneys will become more astute in picking those elements apart and will tap the qualifications of former police managers and trainers to speak for their side.

Here's what I hate to encounter. For example when a state has for over twenty years provided a model policy manual especially tailored for smaller (under 50 officers) agencies, and you are presented in 2013 with a department's pursuit policies devoid of the requisite policy statement, definitions, or treatment of the 20 or so essential components of a policy. The job of the plaintiff's attorney is made easier. Why? Since any executive can download a perfect policy format along with headers, division and sections, with treatment of all critical topics to include a choice of acceptable policy statements asking only for that executive to make the selections, and run the policy off, why not do it? Why go so unprepared and unprotected into the defense? Of course, we have to comment on the fact that through the inadequacies of the policy, the officers are deprived of the administrative guidance that they should have in the performance of their tasks.

In many cases we make it too easy for our opponents. Remember that the one certain means of winning all lawsuits is for the officers' performance to be totally in line with professional standards. That strategy should eliminate the chance of a lawsuit, or if one is filed, the plaintiff's bar should discouraged from pursuing it too vigorously once they are apprised of the strength of our case.

Learning from our experience

I contend that we don't learn enough from our experiences in the legal process. It seems to me that all the lessons are present, the messages resonate from the courts' decisions, and if they were totally learned or heeded, we would decrease the impact of liability. In **Teaching as a Subversive Activity,** Neil Postman once related the story of a teacher who remarked that he had taught the lesson very well, but the students had just not learned it. Postman continued by saying that this is akin to a car salesman saying that he had sold a car but that the customer just didn't buy it. We don't buy the messages that have been so costly for us. We don't learn the lessons to the extent they change our conduct and that of our officers. We don't change our performance enough.

We will only be in a more defensible, possibly almost invulnerable position when are policies cannot be attacked and the training, while superbly documented is state-of-the-art. Finally when supervision consistently supports performance at the highest levels and reacts when it does not meet the accepted standards.

There is a veritable fortune in lessons out there to be learned. We must multiple our efforts to learn those lessons. If they have cost us a lot, let's get our money's worth out of them.

CHAPTER 3

THE OPPOSITION'S GAME PLAN

"To win in the liability arena you have to understand the game plan of the opposition. Their game plan is an open book. There is no secret. Read it and act accordingly to defend yourself."

-Gallagher's Principles #4

"Work smarter, not harder."

-Peter Drucker

While we bemoan the legal assaults of the plaintiff's bar, the police profession has not garnered much knowledge from how it will strengthen its defenses. We pride ourselves on being "trained observers," but in the tumult of handling a myriad number of calls-for-service, crime investigations, and the daily tasks that just patrolling generates, we have neglected to carefully examine the opposition's approach to litigation.

We know why the opposition attacks us. Now we have to get answers. Let me pose two questions:

1. How does the opposition attack us?
2. Where do they concentrate their efforts?

Five Points of Attack

Maybe we can understand more of the approach of the plaintiffs' attorneys when we read in the preface of the National Lawyer's Guild guide for attorneys **Police Misconduct,** which states that:

> "Law enforcement is an impossible task. Police abuse is found in routine performance of police duties. Law enforcement and law observance are often mutually exclusive. Effective attempts to prevent crime lead to excesses which violate legal norms."

Those attorneys see things differently from us. Their perspective is to look for the deficiencies or shortcomings in police actions, and while acknowledging the difficulty of the tasks that officers are called upon to perform, they see violations that for them can blossom into prime targets for lawsuits. Police know that they can enforce the law and observe the law; to achieve that goal, though, we must be completely attentive to the laws that regulate what we can do and what we cannot do, completely attentive to the policies and procedures that represent the standards of our profession. It is a challenging task, but it is not an impossibility.

While we cannot be totally autonomous because we are subject to elected leaders, unless policing exhibits dynamic leadership in combating liability and all that it connotes, external forces will impose directions on our organizations, decreasing the autonomy of the profession. Our first and foremost policy must be so lead and so direct our agencies that there is little cause for other outside forces to intrude. That is our challenge.

The most cursory examinations of the plethora of lawsuits filed against police officers and their departments quickly indicate the plaintiff's Five Points of Attack:

1. **First Point: The Officer Level**
    - everything surrounding the incident:
        - who?
        - what?
        - where?
        - why?
        - circumstances?
        - reasons?
        - subject's actions?
        - officer's reactions?

In police litigation especially in claims of excessive force, the term "totality of the circumstances" will occur, an all-encompassing term meant to take into consideration a wide range of factors covering the subject's demeanor, certain moves that he made, the lighting in the area, his statements, the number of subjects, the physical condition of the officer possibly after a long foot chase, the slipperiness of the ground, weapons displayed, whether the officer was wounded in any way. The term, totality of the circumstances, is meant to convey as much as possible the conditions the officer was facing. The officer's incident report should place the reviewer on the scene in the shoes of the officer as it were.

Too often officers clearly justified in using a certain level of force do not report on the "totality of the circumstances" and leave certain details for a deposition one or two years later. It's hard to say they forgot to put these details in their report and then claim almost total recall years later.

Of course this does not have the same ring of credibility that a more complete incident report would have had, presuming that they read it before the deposition. The quality of the report or lack thereof directly impacts on our ability to defend ourselves in litigation. Even more so, the quality of our officers' reports if not complete as to all the details, might only encourage some attorneys to move forward with a lawsuit. Sure it's up to the officer to fill in all the graphic details, and then for a supervisor to review the report. Possible problem: the supervisor so familiar with similar incidents, can probably from memory conjure up the missing details, and doesn't think of the down-the-road problems their absence here can cause.

In training I used to talk about the "Johnny Cochran Test," named after the now deceased lead attorney in the O.J. Simpson case who was a common opponent in police cases. The Johnny Cochran Test consisted in pretending to have him review our officers' reports. If after he did this and was to remark, "There's nothing for me here," then I would feel it is a good report, and the officer acted appropriately. If only all of our officers' reports would pass this test!

Some lawsuits restrict the range of the complaint to the officer's actions. But that is comparatively rare. In most cases, in the original complaint filed with the court in addition to focusing on the incident itself in which the plaintiff has an encounter with the police, the plaintiff's attorney expands the filed complaint to include other defendants (other officers, the supervisors and quite commonly the chief of police) while naming the jurisdiction itself. He tries to spread the net as wide as possible. Too often in the past seeing the range and magnitude of the complaint, we have settled early on.

There really cannot be a lawsuit without some initial incident involving representatives of the department. A lawsuit cannot be filed exclusively for "deficient policy," "improper training," "constitutional violations" without attaching these charges to a particular incident, or series of incidents.

The original incident allows the plaintiff's attorney to "go over the wall" to attack the department itself, and therefore can expose some of the department's serious and systemic problems.

In an ideal world the completeness and descriptive thoroughness of the report based on the officer's superior performance would be enough to deter any lawsuit except the totally frivolous.

The Points (2-5) of Attack at the Department Level

We find very frequently that in addition to the complaint against the officers, there is that range of additional complaints, not against them but against the functions that the department is responsible for providing to those officers.

Point 2: The Policies

Policies (or lack of them) are always at issue; these policies provided by the department lay out for the officer the performance standards of all tasks relating to the incident itself. There must be a specificity in the plaintiff's request for production of documents from the department's policies, and once the relevant policies are formally requested, the department will eventually have to produce them, or admit that they do not have policies on the topics requested. Regrettably, it is commonplace for officers when deposed to express little knowledge of the policies, losing the opportunity to claim that their actions were guided by the policies.

If officers were totally knowledgeable about the policies, if they could quote, if not chapter and verse, but the import of the relevant policies they might become a more ready guide to their actions on the street. Furthermore, their performance during the deposition might be considerably improved. Often officers' admissions that they are not sure of the components of the policy have them immediately start reflecting on this deficiency, thereby not allowing them to correctly answer subsequent questions.

Point 3: Training

Training will become an issue in the sense that the officer should have been prepared and qualified to perform all the tasks related to the incident. Plaintiffs' attorneys are learning more and more that training can be an important issue bolstering their case. Requests for production of documents will include all basic, Field Training Officer (FTO) records, in-service and specialized training for the officers involved in the incident.

It is my observation that while plaintiff's attorneys are now more likely after the **Canton v. Harris** decision decided almost 25 years ago to go heavy on requesting training documents, they as a group have not learned how to use that material effectively against police defendants. That slight advantage could change quickly. But our mere production of training documents does not offer maximum protection because upon examination they are fraught with gaps, and the officers' qualifications through tests to pass subjects or to show mastery especially in the basic academy when subjected to rigorous educational and training standards will not hold up. As such, hardly any in-service training has any valid testing.

Yes, it is the rare plaintiff's attorney who does more than a perfunctory job at reviewing training documents. Having said that, these attorneys while not pursuing the educational methodologies employed in the training environments, are able to follow the "chain of evidence" when there are repeated recommendations or directives from municipal bodies to check on, review, or change certain practices. Often these bodies require annual reports which the police agency does not produce. In one case they required a video presentation to be made by the chief of police, and it was never produced. Attorneys have examined required roll call training showing it was not focused on the clearly designated problems areas. This total disregard can fashion the basis for "deliberate indifference" on the part of the city according to the **Canton** case and lead to multi-million dollar judgments.

Vast strides have to be made in the training of officers to improve the methodologies and the testing procedures.

Someone once said: "Police training is a process where the notes of the instructor are made the notes of the student or trainee without passing through the minds of either." Sure it's something that provokes a laugh, but there is too much of the truth present. The emphasis is on listening, remembering, and responding in tests but not on ensuring understanding which is the real key to proper decision making.

The process of police training from the basic to the upper levels of in-service training has many deficiencies. How much of what is presented in the academy is really learned? How much goes into long term memory? How much can we actually prove that the officer learned? How can we show competency?

Case in point: defensive tactics. Commonly a defensive tactics instructor will explain a particular hold, will demonstrate it, and then have the class pair off where each one is subjected to the hold. Trainees are chary of not having their partner succeed, and the few repetitions (1-3) do not create enough muscle memory to be able to quickly recall the hold and use it successfully on the street.

For anyone at all familiar with any type of physical training be it defensive tactics, golf or yoga the number of repetitions to embed the process runs to the hundreds or thousands. Most officers will try and stay in shape by weight training and running, but a different attitude must be developed toward the full range of defensive tactics so that there is the confidence in an officer's ability to use them and not immediately resort to a higher level of force too quickly. In saying this I do realize that some officers take the time to stay in shape and to constantly improve all of their defensive tactics, but we cannot rely on just the academy training to accomplish this goal.

Yes, trainers in the academies may be required to take Instructional Design courses and even Train-the-Trainer courses, but that is not universal. We are also quite stingy in the amount of time given to the academy or basic training. Looking at the beginnings of policing in the United States, we find it was strictly O.J.T.; then it was formalized into an academy of a couple of hundred hours. Now it lasts six to nine months. But still is it adequate given the challenge of the tasks we impose on our officers?

Look at the corpus of all the legal training compressed into 60 to even 100 hours. On the basis of this brief exposure to the gamut of all the criminal and civil law that the trainees will eventually be called upon to enforce, these graduates will be out on the street with the best of intentions performing stops, and making arrests.

It would be the truly exceptional academy that has any but objective tests to cover the legal block of training. Yet, the foundation of good performance for that future officer is to know the law, explain why a certain action is taken, and be able to defend that action. Objective tests do not indicate the necessary understanding of the law as a prelude towards report writing. I feel that essay questions applying the law and its elements to the subject's actions would be far better for achieving the goal of better reports and better explanations.

What happens most frequently is that the practical knowledge of the law and its operational demands are learned for the most part by seeing what other officers do. Many officers make great efforts to learn and follow the law, but there are a considerable number on the street that have learned the practical applications, the how-to-do-it, but not the why-we do-it or why-it-should-be-done-this-way and not that way. Are we allowing questionable practices to be passed from one veteran officer to new recruits who sense this is how it is done?

What exists in many basic academies is a tremendously compressed curriculum, trainers who are not really trained adequately themselves in pedagogical techniques and the latest training technologies (or the academy cannot afford them), and who rely on frequent lectures and tests with some practical exercises to cover the blocks of the curriculum in the required time.

If the situation needs drastic upgrading in many basic academies, the post-academy training starting with the Field Training Officer (FTO) program and going to all in-service training must be buttressed. The first experience of training for the new officer immediately follows the academy and is universally called the Field Training Officer (FTO) period, an eight- to twelve-week program of the new officer riding with an experienced, specially training officer with daily and weekly evaluations and the cycling of three FTOs observing the new officer on different shifts during this period.

Properly run, and properly supervised this shines as a veritable solid and undoubtedly valuable period of training. It is based on observations, and on evaluations by different trainers of new officers actually performing the daily routine required on the street. Departments without it are denying their officers and their management an incisive look at how the new officer performs.

Departments having part-time officers, said to be necessary where there is a profusion of small, with 15 or fewer officers, agencies have to be particularly vigilant. It is unlikely that these part-time officers have gone through an FTO program. Incidentally the exposure of these officers is difficult to minimize, given the probability that they might be cobbling together something close to a full-time income by working for several smaller departments, possibly hoping for a full-time position to step into. Why? Can the employing departments keep all of them apprised of the required policies? Can they maintain their qualifications? If employed by several departments, which one is to take responsibility for the necessary recordkeeping and requisite training? One wonders whether with the best of intentions they get confused as to which policy to follow on a given day.

In-service on a myriad number of topics, specialized (as in radar certification), and supervisory training has some excellent courses. That is dependent on the location, academy or the course provider. Certificates are awarded for officers but some are still labeled "for successful completion of a course of three days in ...." Successful completion would require some form of testing which seldom occurs. Certificates now read for "attendance" which is a more accurate comment. Some courses produce officers who are "certified" as taser instructors for example with or without a formal measuring of their grasp of all the issues, practices and procedures necessary to train others.

When demanded through requests for production of documents, departments may produce the certificates and even the lesson plans, but they are not guaranteed to protect the officer and the department. These documents might only expose the gaps in the training.

For example, one of the twelve largest departments in the country, had in its documents in 2008 that they were still teaching **Johnson v. Glick**, the forerunner to **Graham v. Connor** and had that case and its incorrect principles solidly put forth in its Use of Force policy written in 2000, a full twelve years after the **Graham** decision in effect changed the legal requirements for legitimate uses of force!

My point in all this is to alert you to what I see as a renewed and intense scrutiny of all training relating to what I would call the High Risk/Critical Tasks, those that produce 90-95% of all liability arising from police activity. We'll see more on this later.

Point 4: Supervision

Discussing supervision I am reminded that a number of years ago, when a group of police chiefs from the largest jurisdictions in this country were queried about their greatest internal problem, the answer was unanimous: "The quality of first line supervision."

The reach of the police chief to effect change on the operational level is limited by the quality of first line supervision. It must be realized that the training of police supervisors starts with their first day on the job, when they are exposed to a supervisor, for from there on they are picking up cues on how that position is performed, for better or for worse.

Traditionally supervisors are not trained prior to the assumption of this critically important position. Many are already promoted to this rank when they get their first chance to attend any type of supervisory class which might only last two or three days. With no training their style of supervision may already have been formed. Promotion should not precede training and the assumption of that new position's responsibilities.

More importantly supervisors stand with a foot in two worlds. They come from the officer ranks, and possibly for years they have worked side-by-side with their fellow officers; then they are promoted. The department is asking for a tremendous change in their perception of performance; even their buddies see them in a different light.

What style of supervision do they adopt? How do they make sure policies are followed? How do they counsel, or even reprimand the officers? How do they evaluate them and their performance? How do they handle those RODS, officers "retired on duty?" And on it goes. First line supervisors are faced with a greater variety of challenging problems than any other rank.

The challenge for many is insurmountable and they become more passive when they should have acted, they overlook actions that are out of policies or contrary to procedures, and which they should correct. Or performance adhering to departmental values, policies and procedures may just stay constant, never improving, or it can slide down forming a greater gap between actual performance and those standards.

Point 5: Discipline and corrective action

Especially when there is the suspicion of a series of incidents similar to the one which has occasioned the lawsuit, plaintiff's attorneys will look for disciplinary or corrective action on the part of the administration where the involved officer had been found disobeying policies and procedures in the past.

The previous incidents have placed the administration on notice that the officer has a problem. (How do you defend an agency when an officer generated five complaints in his second year on the department which was surpassed by seven in his second year? True, few were sustained but all had elements of uses of force, the common element. In sixteen years he averaged over one complaint annually. This pattern culminated in two very serious uses of force with no record of any intervention on the part of the agency.)

With discernible patterns we would ask if there was progressive discipline involved in which the repetition of these acts resulted in more heavier discipline? Furthermore, the particular pattern of activity might be more common among a group of officers, perhaps on the midnight shift. What was the action taken by the administration? Did the administration track on these officers?

If the administration knew about the problem, did it take actions commensurate with its severity? Probably the most desirable outcome for the plaintiff's attorney is to find that in addition to the alleged misconduct exhibited by the officer in this incident, there was a number of complaints of similar activity by this officer or others, and no steps were initiated by the administration. It would be a classic case of "knew or should have known" broadening and solidifying the complaint against the department.

Points 2-5 Are Controllable

With good management and supervision, Points of Attack 2-5, policy, training, supervision and discipline, are controllable by the department. With time all of these critical factors can be improved and brought up to professional standards.

That would leave Point 1. The incident itself is not totally controllable, that is, the interaction between what should be a well-trained officer with the appropriate direction through policy, procedures and training as to how to confront this situation, how to deal with this particular subject. However, the better the administration has brought points 2-5 up to standards, the more chances that:

1. the officer will deal with the subject appropriately;
2. the lower the possibility, regardless of how the officer deals with the subject, that the plaintiff's attorney can make any real headway in expanding the case through the policy, training, supervision and discipline routes.

We have to ask the question: "What does the plaintiff's attorney concentrate on?" The response is easy: the attorney will focus on the low level performance, actions taken by officers that are apparently short of professional standards, against departmental policies and accepted procedures.

To reduce litigation our response is easy: raise the level of performance of our officers so there are fewer opportunities for an attorney to file a lawsuit. Deny these attorneys the raw material on which to craft a suit. Make the interactions between citizens and officers devoid as much as humanly possible of anything that could foster a suit.

In other words, concentrate on high level performance in every interaction. To win against plaintiffs' attorneys the proven presence of that level of performance is the key, so that every place where an attack might be made, i.e. on policy, training, supervision and discipline and corrective action, there is no separation from the highest performance levels.

A logical conclusion is that the plaintiff's attorney uses the activating incident to initiate the action against the department. We know the opposition's game plan. We know where the attacks in civil proceedings will originate. We know we can buttress our defenses by working carefully to bring policy, training, supervision and discipline/corrective action up to the profession's highest standards. We then stand an excellent chance of not only all but eliminating suits, but in winning the diminished number that might be filed.

In the course of this litigation gauntlet, it is common to see the suit filed against the officers, a supervisor, and the police executive. In the run up to the trial, through the drawn out process of discovery which would include production of documents, depositions by both sides, and experts' reports, frequently the police executive may be dropped from the lawsuit.

The named officers are originally bolstered by the presence of the police executive; they now feel abandoned, thinking that massive legal efforts rescued the executive leaving them in the suit by themselves. In many cases officers do not realize that the defense strategies for the officers are markedly different from that of the executive. The necessary legal proof to show that the executive was "deliberatively indifferent," or that there existed a policy or custom of allowing excessive force or some other action relevant to the case is never satisfactorily established through the discovery process.

Speaking frankly, the effort to pin liability on the executive follows a different course of action and is quite challenging for the plaintiff's attorney, who thwarted in the attempts to saddle the department with successful charges, retreats to the original complaint where all his efforts are focused on the officers. The defense attorney can submit motions for the dropping of the executive because in the original complaint the plaintiffs expanded their claims but subsequently made no further progress through production of documents, through their expert's reports, nor finally through depositions to make their case any stronger.

A couple of points

When the jury's verdict is in, remember that not all losses are directly the result of the actions of the officers in the street. Sometimes the jury will be swayed by evidence produced about the shortcomings of the department itself. Sometimes the marginal performance of the officers is tainted by the failure of the department; the case which could go either way for plaintiff or defense is lost by the inadequacy of the department's four points: policy, training, supervision or discipline. Sometimes defense attorneys will recommend a settlement when they want to choke off damaging testimony that might enlarge the final judgment in the eyes of the jury.

Profit from the department's experience in a suit and especially in court. Learn from the alleged weaknesses exposed during the litigation. Get feedback for your department from the legal proceedings. Learn furthermore from the liability experience of other departments in your region. Go over and discuss with them the legal involvements; gather any type of information that will help your department.

Thousands of years ago, SunTsu, the great Chinese strategist wrote in **The Art of War** the oft-quoted maxim summarized as follows:

> "Know yourself and your enemy and you will win every battle.
> Know yourself but not the enemy, you will win some and lose some.
> If you don't know yourself and you don't know the enemy, you will lose every battle."

So let us truly be trained observers; let us understand exactly how the plaintiffs' attorneys will come after us, and deny them the critical points of attack. Knowing their strategy and knowing our strengths, we will more likely win our legal battles.

CHAPTER 4

HANDLING POLICE PERFORMANCE DATA

> "Police gather data on performance, and plaintiffs' attorneys analyze them."
>
> -Gallagher's Principles #25

Police are action-oriented, but they do record mounds of reports of all of their activities. While not stored in filing cabinets any more, a computer disc loaded with performance data can pierce the protective shell of an organization and expose its inner workings.

I can remember as director of public safety overseeing a fairly large police (240 officers) and fire (210 firefighters) departments speaking with the respective chiefs about their annual reports. For years the police had faithfully recorded the number of patrol miles driven as a form of accomplishment; on the fire side they had recorded the number of gallons pumped and the number of miles of hoses laid. There was absolutely no connection between these figures in their annual reports and the real attainments of their departments. With a stolid reluctance they acceded to my directives and dropped these figures, but were hard pressed to come up with new performance numbers until we sat down and looked for better indicators of actual operations toward their stated goals.

Police generally don't work well with statistics and data; all too often the data are not used for any relevant management decisions. Yet the proper utilization of data, analyzed correctly, can direct management to make better decisions. Not using data analysis adequately, deprives management of critical insights into the workings of the department and their individual officers.

Furthermore, the failure to perform this critical analysis of gathered data, commonly places the department and its executives on the defensive when there is an incident. Through discovery the records having the data are disclosed to the plaintiff's attorney. If what has been handed over, and subsequently analyzed by the opposition is then served up in depositions of department executives, it can clearly indicate that they had the opportunity (and also the obligation) to make use of that data. They either knew about the conclusions that could be drawn from the data, and did nothing; or they had an obligation to analyze the very data so available in their computers, but did not.

Edwards Deming and Performance Data

Edwards Deming, the quality consultant who did so much to lift post-war Japan and its industry to high quality levels, presented us with two principles if we want quality performance:

1. Gather and analyze data:
2. Understand that process problems create people problems.

Deming would have us as departmental administrators look to the basis for any suits even if we eventually prevail, to look for patterns, and identify processes that might be contributing to the problem. Deming would have us ask ourselves four questions:

1. What data should we be gathering?
2. What data should we be analyzing?
3. What should we do with the data?
4. What needs to be improved? Changed? Done away with?

If our goal is quality, high level performance to avoid liability, then anything that gives us an insight into performance is extremely important. We must of course be selective in the data we gather and the data that we analyze.

Witness Sir George Pickering's astute comment:

> "Not everything that counts can be counted and not everything that is counted, counts."

Any management worth its salt, like any successful business has to make decisions based on data gathered and analyzed. To fail to do this is to fail as a business, or in policing to fail to use resources properly, to fail at being as effective as we should be, to fail to have in place the adequate defensive postures, to fail to be successful in litigation as often as we should. The conclusions are obvious: data with ongoing analysis are invaluable for the success we all want.

Let's address Deming's second principle. Too often police management may take action, and separate an individual from the department. The fallacy is that the problem has disappeared, (a classic case of out-of-sight-out-of-mind). Because we see the problem limited to the individual, we think we no longer have to worry about it. Wrong according to Deming and rightly so.

The problem officer even terminated from the department is sending us a message that we may have faulty processes in place. We did not hire him because we thought he would be a potential problem. We vetted him extensively and thought we had the best of candidates for an open officer position. But some combination of circumstances in the course of his career with the agency generated a problem, or possibly it was the officer's reaction to certain circumstances that transformed someone whom we thought a great prospect into a problem officer.

The process problems might be our training, the inadequacy of supervision or our failure to recognize the earliest stages of the problem and take immediate action. Maybe it was some of the officers already on the department, on his shift, that affected his performance in such a manner that this officer found it easier to go over the line into the lower levels of performance. In combination these process failures contributed to their becoming problem officers.

Now, Deming reminds us, if we do nothing when the problem officer leaves, if we do not get the message and examine certain processes, we leave them in place only to have them infect other officers. We leave in place the very process that contributed to the departed officer's problems. The virus continues to spread. Is it surprising that we might have more personnel problems? Do we wonder when we continue to have the same problems year after year?

While there is this reluctance to gather and analyze statistics and data, the world around is replete with the presence of a lot of data mainly concerning sports figures and their accomplishments. Would we enjoy football, basketball or baseball as much as we do if there were not comparisons between players and teams on points like yards per carry, percentage of completed passes, three point shots made, batting average, runs batted in, strikeouts per game, or earned run averages. The movie "Moneyball" brought out the value of statistics and the correlation with performance. While not every police activity can be reduced to statistical analysis, that analysis if resulting in needed changes can allow us to field a more productive organization, and one less likely to have to shoulder today's burden of liability.

Analysis of performance data is critical to exposing problems such as patterns of excessive use of force, problems specific to one shift, the quality of supervision, or the pattern of questionable arrests. Some examples will follow.

1. Data on possible racial profiling

Numerous departments have been accused of racial profiling, concentrating enforcement activities on minorities. One method of examining an officer's arrest patterns or even that of an entire shift would be to scrutinize traffic stops and the purported justifications for these stops. An extreme example for illustrative purposes: if 100% of an officer's stops are of minorities then we might conclude that there is racial profiling.

But examining the reason for the stops might cast the citations/arrests in a different light. If every stop and subsequent arrest was basically a non-discretionary action, i.e. the car was stolen, the car had been involved in a hit-and-run, the officer recognized the driver as being wanted for a felony, it is hard to call it profiling. However, if 100% of the stops and arrests were for discretionary reasons, i.e. improper lane change, 55 m.p.h. in 45 m.p.h. zone, or not slowing completely at a stop sign, then there is more of a basis for the charge.

Obviously traffic stops by one officer or all officers on a shift would not be 100% one way or the other, but the data on the reasons for traffic stops would signal if there is a need for further investigation. Over and above that it would allow the department to present a logical defense of its actions on one hand, or to take prompt corrective action on the other if questioned by the city council or by reporters. Defend yourself with the data, but have them on hand, ready to use.

With the onset of serious concerns over sexual misconduct by officers, this type of review to look at the sex of the persons being pulled over might lead to an indication of an incipient problem. If most or all of the stops are totally discretionary and most or all of the stops are of females by male officers, then it bears looking into.

2. The shooting of dogs by police

Police officers are often faced with considerable personal danger when enforcing the law, and when serving warrants. Certain unsavory locations might be defended by ferocious dogs which menace or attack officers when they are legally entering a property. Or possibly they have to respond when citizens alert them to the dangers they face with a vicious dog in the neighborhood.

One major city was castigated in the media because of shooting a dog on of all days, Christmas Eve. The dog, a boxer, was off leash contrary to the jurisdiction's regulations in a large playground behind a school at midnight when an officer checking out the location, spotted a car parked toward the rear of the building. Upon investigating the boxer ran at him while he shouted for the owner to call him off. The dog came running at a speed which for a boxer could reach 44' per second. The officer fired one shot when the dog was a few feet away fatally wounding the animal.

The press as it is wont to do dug up other instances of officers shooting dogs, portraying their actions as uncalled for to say the least. A lawsuit was filed which asked for an astronomical amount of money, claiming there was a pattern or policy of needlessly shooting dogs. While suffering from a rash of negative articles concerning their actions, the department realized it had ten years of records of dogs shot by police. There never had been any statistics accumulated and certainly not analyzed on this activity over the decade.

Working from those files for over 110 incidents, I was able to show 100% of the shootings involved the ten most dangerous breeds of dogs; 74% were pit bulls. There were fewer shootings per officer than in other large cities, 80% were at night, 36% were in the vestibules of houses, 37% were during the service of warrants, 22% in response to reported dog attacks on persons, and officers fired 1.1 rounds per incident far fewer than other major cities. With guidance from a national animal protective group, the city fathers wanted officers to use pepper spray first and only resort to deadly force if the spray was ineffective. Data showed that officers would never have been able to use the spray in close quarters, or shift to their weapon if needed.

With the analysis of the available, but previously untouched records, the picture conveyed was of officers responsibly using their weapons to protect themselves or others, and not capriciously as was hinted at in the press. The plaintiff's attorney, seeing the data analysis folded his case.

It is not known whether the department having been successful in its defense, learned the value of keeping updated statistics. Are the shootings of dogs tracked annually by breed, circumstances, location, number of shots fired, time of day, and reason for the call or the need for the warrant service? Be proactive for the data offer an essential protection for the department if not from a lawsuit, then from unneeded criticism in the press.

Now most departments in suburban areas will not experience a problem of this magnitude or criticality. The officers' need to take action against dogs might not even occur. But the lesson is present: data and subsequent analysis can be our protection.

3. Data employed against police

In a large metropolitan police agency, a disorderly conduct arrest based on disturbing the peace by loud and boisterous noise at night was made a *cause célèbre* as various groups protested the allegedly specious bases for these arrests. During the course of discovery plaintiffs requested and received arrest reports for this very offense for a six-month period. One of the elements of the offense is that it had to be committed at night.

The opposition's analysis of this mound of performance data on this one discrete task brought out the fact that close to 25% of the arrests were made during the daylight hours, and all of the arrest reports were approved by supervisors. (The plaintiff's expert even took the trouble of factoring in the recorded times of sunrise and sunset into his calculations.)

Certainly through inadequate supervision and review of the arrest reports, the mistake went unnoticed until forces aligned behind this particular arrest and lawsuit brought it to the fore along with the mass of previous arrests. Admittedly 25% of those arrests in the six-month period reviewed by the plaintiffs were illegal, not meeting the elements of the statute.

Consider the burden to the department over the possibility of the massive number of suits for false arrest. A proper review done conscientiously by supervisors would have promptly rejected these arrests. Or even one supervisor who noticed the trend could have alerted higher ups to prod them into action. The net result is a judgment for a hefty amount for the arrestee and literally millions for the law firm in conjunction with the ACLU, that pursued the case for close to five years.

Did the department learn from this costly encounter to change policies, to train officers and supervisors in the correct application of the statute, to require additional scrutiny of every future arrest for this offense? That we don't know, but it would be the appropriate response to salvage some benefits from this economically pyrrhic event.

4. Supervising traffic stops

One agency under a federal consent decree, a decree initiated mainly because of questionable traffic stops involving minorities was required by the decree to take extensive steps to bring this activity into conformity with constitutional requirements. A lengthy checklist was filled out on every traffic stop requiring data on the vehicle description, race of the driver, occupants, reason for a search, written consent for a search, notice of right to refuse, search of persons and whether any force was used. This of course was combined with explicit training on these requirements.

Since every police car has a dashcam, every stop was recorded and this was matched by supervisors against the reports. The supervisors' efforts and the dashcam videos were randomly reviewed by the federal monitoring team which over time reported on the correctness of the supervisors in evaluating "good" stops. Through these constant efforts the percentage of correct stops rose slightly at first and then more dramatically. The final result was that in one monitoring period for all the stops reviewed by the team, 100% were perfectly performed. It was then attested that the department was in complete compliance with the relevant standard.

Now this achievement occurred with a lot of attention paid to this task. The department deserves credit for its attainment of individual and near corporate perfection. It goes without saying that once the extra attention of the monitors was removed, was the quality of supervision such that this level was maintained over time? That would be the real test.

But there are obvious lessons to be garnered from the experience of this department. They are:

1. clearly defined standards, policies and procedures,
2. accompanied by strict performance goals,
3. with training to incorporate all of the administration's expected outcomes,
4. with exacting supervisory oversight and analysis of performance data,
5. coupled with necessary retraining when necessary
6. will produce dramatic results.

Note: with the proliferation of dashcams on patrol cars I note a reluctance to say the least, about the regular review of a random sample of these videos by supervisors. In many cases, reviews only take place when there is a complaint or a lawsuit. Supervisors cannot be at the scene of an incident for every one of their officers, but the dashcam allows them to observe how the task was performed giving them an excellent perspective on performance.

The lesson is obvious: it is foolish not to employ these videos to evaluate officer conduct on a regular basis, and not only when there is trouble. Most officers handle these challenging assignments superbly; supervisors should use those reviews as chances to commend officers for it is proof of the policies and training being followed correctly.

Progress at what cost?

You know that we hate to admit it, but the police profession has made progress as the result of the pressures applied by lawsuits. We have been coerced into taking certain steps either from lawsuits we have lost, or possibly from the examples of other agencies' traumatic experiences in court.

But the question posed should be: "Would we rather move forward by reaching for and grasping higher standards of documented performance or move forward by being kicked in the rear by litigation?" I would certainly opt for the former myself and I am sure you would also.

A final word about Deming

We've seen his first two principles, "gather and analyze data," and "look to the process problems that causes people problems." We should not neglect the third one, which to many would seem far removed from the first two. To Edwards Deming, to achieve quality performance he adds a necessary factor: "There must be joy in the workplace."

This begs the question: Are the working environments of our police departments conducive to making all personnel happy? Is it possible for a police organization to have personnel who are happy in their work? Joyful? Satisfied? Are personnel energized with a sense of self-worth, or contributing in a purposeful manner to the onward progress of the organization? Are they respected and given a chance to grow professionally and yes, personally?

Policing services will always be provided through formal organizations that currently are struggling with the burden of liability in addition to stressful workloads. Litigation has become more of an issue when police officers launch suits against their supervisors in their own departments. (Is this increase in suits filed by our own personnel against the management of their organizations a commentary on the manner in which the department is run?)

Does it say something about the leadership? The absence of clearly articulated values that guide actions at all levels? The way I see it, if we are truly interested in decreasing liability, processes can be put in place to achieve that decrease to a great extent of the burden of liability. Then I think we will arrive at about 75% of establishing an effective organization.

The next elevation will come with great leadership, solid management, with clearly defined organizational values, vision and a pronounced mission that penetrates all actions. If the expressed values permeate the organization can the organization become value-guided rather than policy-driven? At this level we would achieve 85% of that which makes for an effective organization. The ultimate step would be to make the workplace a sanctuary and community characterized by people being respected for their contributions, working purposefully and growing and living daily on the job. That effort gets us to the 90-95% level.

Too often we hear officers saying how they can't wait to get through their five days of work so that they can really live on the weekend or their days off. They endure the work so they can merit the weekend, to restore their emotional, psychic and physical energies.

I feel, and I must admit this is by far the ideal situation, that a workplace can be a place of growth, that people can work together. The mission of police is commonly stated as "to protect and serve." I commonly ask whom are you protecting and serving. The ready answer is the "community." My response is: "Which community?"

There are two communities: the external one of the citizens and the internal one of all the personnel in the department. I state that there must be protection and service internally from the top to the bottom of the organization, for one imbued with these characteristics will be better suited to do the same for the external community. This is the level of the organization at 95% of its effectiveness.

If we were assessing the level of different departments, and if you can accept my three gradations awarding a 70-75% to those effectively fending off liability, awarding an 80-85% to those with solid leadership with mission, vision and values made operational, and 90-95% to those which are both communities and sanctuaries, that there is a form of joy in that workplace, then there will be steady, consistent quality performance, and achievement of our ultimate goal.

CHAPTER 5

PLACING THE EMPHASIS: THE HIGH RISK/CRITICAL TASKS

"Peak performers are not ordinary people with something added. They are ordinary people with nothing taken away."
-<u>Peak Performers</u> by Charles Garfield

"A person's and an organization's objective must lie not in the futile efforts towards the accommodation of man to the circumstances in which he finds himself, but in the maintenance of a kind of candid discontent in the face of the highest achievement."
-Walter Pater

"The quickest way to kill the human spirit is to ask someone to do mediocre work."
-Ayn Rand

It is important to achieve early results and possibly major ones at that, the departmental defenses be strengthened to the utmost degree to improve performance in the High Risk/Critical Tasks (HR/CTs), the ones most likely to end in litigation as a result of police actions or the most difficult to perform or the ones that have caused a major problem in the community. Mostly those that have serious liability potential.

What are the High Risk/Critical Tasks? Well, they are as mentioned above, the ones most likely to generate complaints, claims and lawsuits. Is the list ironbound? No, certainly not. Administrators in giving police powers to any sworn officers realize that certain HR/CTs will remain the same across the board, while a few of those tasks will be different because of special responsibilities imbedded in those departments or because of the special nature of the department.

Since the late 1990s I have worked on emphasizing the HR/CTs usually suggesting just twelve, although any agency might desire to include some additional ones. In the last few years, the members of the Police Executive Research Forum (PERF) at one of their conferences listed the issues that might generate attention from the Department of Justice and their investigative responsibility. Those issues were: uses of force, biased policies, unlawful vehicle stops and arrests, searches, gender bias in handling sexual assaults, and police interventions with persons having some form of mental illness.

They are included here, not because we are trying to avoid a DOJ investigation, but to avoid involvement in lawsuits. All of the tasks that would attract the attention of DOJ according to the PERF membership are included on my list of HR/CTs developed in 1995 from a perspective of avoiding liability.

My suggestions for the list of HR/CTs are as follows:

1. The use of force
2. Pursuits
3. Emergency operations of police vehicles
4. Search and seizure and arrest
5. Care, custody, restraints and transportation of prisoners
6. Domestic violence to include agency personnel
7. Officer off-duty conduct and limits of authority
8. Sexual harassment and sexual misconduct of officers
9. Selection, appointment, and failure to terminate
10. Complaint process and Internal Affairs
11. Special operations, narcotics units, high risk warrants and undercover assignments
12. Dealing with the mentally ill, emotionally disturbed persons and those with diminished capacity

Departments exclusively focused on traffic control might select another topic rather than domestic violence. A college police department might substitute for special operations the enforcement of alcohol regulations. So the number comes out to about twelve; it could be higher, but prior litigation experience and special tasks germane to the specific police department might dictate changing a few of the HR/CTs. The idea is to keep the number low.

First, once the list of HR/CTs has been determined the policies for those tasks must be updated to rank with the best professional standards. Officers must be trained in those policies relevant to the HR/CTs. Performance short of the standards or policies, or any actions contravening training must be recognized; remediation must be arranged and in some cases discipline must be imposed.

First line supervisors must give special attention to any reports relating to the HR/CTs. Second level supervisors might be required to review those reports also. Those reports found at either level not to be complete must be returned for revision.

Finally the policies associated with the HR/CT policies are "need to know" while all other are "need to reference." Officers have to prove that they know these policies, the "need to know." We would recommend abolishing the fiction that every officer should know every policy. The policymakers don't know all their own policies.

There will no attempt made here to provide recommendations for all the policies relating to the HR/CTs. What follows will be brief commentaries on the twelve HR/CTs selected for our list.

1. The Use of Force

There should be universal agreement on a number of the HR/CTs and this is certainly one of them. Most force policies have something called the "Continuum of Force" explaining that in response to a subject's actions an officer is justified in using a particular level of force. The progression goes from officer presence, to verbal commands, to soft hands, to pepper spray, to Electronic Control Device (Taser), to hard hands, to impact weapons (baton, PR-24, or ASP, retractable striking weapon) and finally to deadly force.

The threefold test of **Graham v. Connor** should be highlighted with an emphasis on officers' reports detailing the totality of the circumstances under which they found that force had to be employed.

Some departments have started to eliminate the Continuum of Force only to emphasize the **Graham** three-fold test of objective reasonableness based on the severity of the crime at issue, whether the subject poses an immediate threat to the safety of officers and others, and finally whether the subject is actively resisting arrest or attempting to evade arrest by flight. (For more on this point see the excellent article by John Klein and Ken Wallentine "A Rational Foundation for Use of Force Policy, Training and Assessment" in the American for Effective Law Enforcement newsletter for July 2014.)

The purpose in this step is to place greater emphasis on the articulation by officers in providing a comprehensive picture of everything they faced which led up to the decision/necessity to use a certain level of force.

2. Pursuits

Pursuits are the active attempts by officers to control/stop drivers who refuse to obey an officer's signal to pull over. Or a pursuit is initiated by an active attempt to evade/elude an officer for some type of serious traffic or criminal offense.

There must be a clear policy statement from the policymaker (the chief executive) that the department's policy falls into three categories. The policy could be discretionary, allowing officers to make any decision about initiating a pursuit based on their judgment. Secondly, the policy could be restrictive in that a pursuit can only be initiated for certain offenses, say serious misdemeanors or felonies. It might not allow a pursuit for a non-continuing traffic offense like running a stop sign. The final type of policy statement could make all pursuits prohibited; no pursuits for any reason. While some departments did at one time adopt this policy, it was rescinded after a short time.

3. Emergency Operation of Vehicles

To some it might seem duplicative and they could argue persuasively that this should not be a standalone HR/CT; it should be folded in under #2 Pursuit. Another alternative would be to have an "emergency vehicle operations" policy and place pursuit under that heading. Those decisions are at the discretion of the policymaker.

I chose to separate them because there is an essential difference between the two tasks. In emergency vehicle operations the officer has to go from point A to point B as quickly and as safely as possible. Officers control the task appreciably more, since they know the destination and can make decisions about the route. In a pursuit on the contrary the officer is going from point A, where the pursuit was initiated to some unknown location. I have characterized this difference to the analogy that in a pursuit the "officer is tied on to the bumper of the car being chased."

My choice was to bifurcate the two tasks and their policies. Usually there is some limit placed on "going code" with lights and sirens. While there might be some distinctions between different states as to the requirements, some might only require visible warning devices, other states require visible and audible warning devices, I argue that both should be activated since the task is fraught with danger to officers, motorists and pedestrians regardless of the state requirement.

In this day of dashcams which are activated when the lights and siren are turned on, we have the means of reviewing every one of these dangerous activities to ascertain if officers made the proper decisions and followed the policies. Some dashcams can give the actual speed of the police car along with the braking action second by second. Dashcams are readily used to justify the driving of the officer or to show what are alleged mistakes in judgment when there is a lawsuit. (It seems an obvious oversight to have dashcams in marked patrol cars and not place them in unmarked cars with lights and sirens used primarily for traffic enforcement.)

However, the use of dashcams to review police performance on a regular basis without some untoward event happening is not too prevalent. If we are interested in the quality of police performance here is incontrovertible proof of the highest level of performance or anything short of that objective. Therefore, it would be better to review the dashcams for all pursuits, some emergency responses and traffic stops.

4. Search, Seizure and Arrests

Probably no task is so subject to legal decisions coming down from appellate courts than anything relating to search, seizure and subsequent arrests. Any case law from state courts and certainly federal courts must be scrutinized for how they might affect the manner in which officers conduct searches and seizures of property and persons.

The event of a neighboring department's involvement in a lawsuit with a subsequent judgment against it should be recognized as an "educable moment," a time when any department can learn from the possibly costly experience of another agency. Once again scrutiny of officers' reports must be thorough; questions must be raised if any part seems out of line with recent decisions. This of course presupposes that the first line supervisors are themselves well versed in the demands of the law.

Knowledge of recent court decisions should be minimally learned as to how the tasks of officers in the street are affected: Is their job made easier? Or is it made harder? What changes are allowed or mandated by the new court decision? This legal direction should be available to the officers in a timely manner, not relegated to "annual legal updates" if that does occur.

5. Care, Custody, Restraints and Transportation of Prisoners

Officers have to realize that once someone is taken into custody, and placed in restraints in the back of a police car, that the officer and the department have assumed almost total responsibility for the person's welfare. They have to make decisions about any form of medical attention required, and the possible justification for additional restraints while avoiding hogtying,

There is always the question of seatbelts. Someone who has taken the efforts of a number of officers to get him into the back seat might not be cooperative in allowing the officer to reach in front of him to fasten the seatbelt. I prefer the language that indicates that all subjects shall be seat belted as long as officer safety is not impinged upon. Some subjects might continually try to bite the officers, or spit on them as they adjust the seat belt.

6. Domestic Violence to Include Agency Personnel

State laws have eliminated the old way of dealing with domestic violence, telling the husband or the male to take a walk and cool off. Now there is mandatory arrest for the primary aggressor. Admittedly these events while frequently occurring are among the hardest tasks placed on the shoulders of the officers because of the difficulty in sorting out the different stories and assessing the identity of that primary aggressor. The task is fraught with danger for the officers themselves.

More challenging is the occasional domestic violence call in which one of the parties is a police officer, possibly belonging to the responding department. Too often there are some special allowances in these situations. However, officers personally involved in a domestic violence incident should be treated the same as any other similar incident although most policies require that a police supervisor be called to the scene. There are obvious implications for the officer's career if convicted due to the prohibition of carrying a weapon.

7. Officer Off-Duty Conduct and Limits of Authority

With a number of "friendly fire" deaths of police officers much needed attention has been accorded the situations where off-duty officers are involved. Quite often under the wording of policies that officers are "on duty 24/7" or "officers may carry their weapon when off duty" there is a definite lack of clarity in the expectations that the department has for the officers as far as limiting their authority when off-duty.

Some policies on this topic tell the officer that he may not carry his weapon off-duty when he has been consuming alcoholic beverages. The implications are plain: the prohibition only kicks into effect after the officer has been drinking. The wording should prohibit the consumption of alcoholic beverages if the officer intends to consume alcohol.

The conditions when an officer is allowed to exercise authority off-duty must be clear. Without radio, OC, or baton the only weapon available is the gun, which might not be appropriate and reasonable in the totality of the circumstances. Off-duty officers shall not take action when they are personably involved as in an argument between neighbors. Once a clear policy is written and officers are trained in its application, there should be scenario-based training on a series of situations that clarify the departmental directives.

8. Selection, Appointment, Part-Timers and Failure to Terminate

Despite our best efforts we end up with some problem officers. If we could foresee that they would become problems we would not appoint them. The best vetting procedures in the world will not bring to the surface the possible psychological issues that might only be exacerbated by policing itself and/or the deterioration occurring in the officer's personal life. So it remains that there should be no stinting on the efforts to discern the best prospects for the basic training and future appointment of sworn officers.

Sometimes we place enduring reliance on the psychological examination given to academy recruits. In today's world there are many factors that will change an officer's attitudes and psychological outlook on life and the job. There must be provisions for fitness for duty examinations when appropriate.

The academies in basic training are chary of dropping a large number of recruits for academic or personal shortcomings. Academy directors are usually subject to the chiefs in the area and shorthanded departments desperately need the additional officers. To drop someone means that department might be short of personnel for another six months or more.

It is unfortunate that smaller departments do not have sufficient staffing to cover all their shifts with full-time personnel. Therefore they hire part-time officers who might be working part-time for a couple of departments amassing part-time incomes for full-time support. Most of these part-time officers are ardently hoping for some agency in the area to offer them a full-time slot. The advantage to the hiring agency is that the officer can start work immediately, and the smaller jurisdiction does not have to expend funds to pay a recruit while he/she goes through the academy.

Because of the complex employment rules police chiefs are hesitant to terminate officers even for just cause because of prolonged appeals which commonly end in reinstatement with back pay to the officer they have deemed not fit for the department. Sometimes these reinstatements are the result of an inadequate preparation and presentation of the department's side in any hearing or appeal of the termination. It is found the department's case is weakened by no documented efforts at remediation, no paper trail of evaluations documenting inadequacies and shortcomings, and no sufficiency in "building a case" for termination.

In other situations officers are allowed to resign rather than be terminated; they move on to another department. The former departments provide a neutral statement of their capabilities and the problem officers move on, becoming in some cases "gypsy cops." For the new agencies that officer might be a liability time bomb.

9. Complaint Process and Internal Affairs

The manner in which the complaint process has been handled over the years and the quality of the Internal Affairs function are ripe ground for plaintiffs' attorneys. I have said: "Police departments gather statistics and plaintiffs' attorneys analyze them." Analyzing complaints and the findings of the Internal Affairs unit offers much to the opposition in building and reinforcing a case against police.

In New Jersey, the ACLU organized a survey of most of the police departments in the state, inquiring about the process of filing a complaint against police. The published results were a massive and almost universal critique about the manner in which complaints were processed if they were even recorded. The N.J. Attorney General on the heels of the ACLU report promulgated a stricter policy for all police departments and established certain requirements for these agencies to file with county prosecutor's offices data on complaints and uses of force.

While Internal Affairs data will not make it into every lawsuit, when it is discovered the results showing percentages of sustained complaints might indicate an extremely low percentage. Further study might show that the complaints of minorities have never been sustained. In a **Monell** type case these data and the accompanying analysis might lend substantial support to a "custom, usage and practice" complaint against the department and the city.

10. Special Operations, Narcotics Units, High Risk Warrants and Undercover Assignments

The mix of activities under this heading constitutes tasks which are infrequent but which have a high degree of criticality. They also demand an intensive amount of training, something that cannot be left entirely to on-the-job training. Not that every police officer is safe on the streets if he or she is in uniform, but these assignments are linked to more frequent injuries of officers, more frequent uses of force, and more dangers to officers and incidentally more lawsuits.

While there are policies relevant to some of these activities, not everything is covered in the manual. It is suggested that these special units work at developing their own policies, subject to the approval of the chief executive. Where possible checklists should be made up so that critical actions will not be overlooked. The checklists also may assist in orienting new members to the teams. These activities to varying degrees are subject to some form of pre-planning to lower the chances of anything going wrong.

Finally there is always the consideration of not leaving a good narcotics or undercover officer in the position for too long for this may contribute to some serious problems.

11. Dealing with the Mentally Ill, Emotionally Disturbed Persons and those With Diminished Capacity

These persons present particular difficulty to responding officers in that they have to protect themselves, they have to enforce the law and take violators into custody and also provide for the needs of the person who is mentally ill, disturbed or who has some diminished capacity.

Officers are not psychologists; they cannot easily diagnose a person's mental state, but they have to be prepared through policies and some training as to their reactive stances. Many larger departments have established Crisis Intervention Teams (CIT teams) who are composed of specially trained officers. At the incident, first arriving officers must be sensitized as to the conditions under which they call for the CIT team realizing that it might be some time before members arrive. In other situations they might have a negotiator on call while the officers do all that they can to contain the situation.

Under this topic officers will occasionally have to confront the person wanting a suicide-by-cop incident. Justification for any force used, especially deadly force must be carefully documented.

A Baker's Dozen

Of course, you do not have to limit your emphasis to these twelve, or to just twelve. But the idea is to focus on what will bring the most immediate return in improved performance on tasks which are the common target of lawsuits. Having said that, in reading an article by John J. Knoll "Dealing with an Armed Populace – Suspect Control in the Age of Open and Concealed Carry" in the May 2014 issue of **The Police Chief** the author poses the problem conveyed in his title: the parameters under which officers develop reasonable suspicion for a stop or probable cause to support an arrest when someone is carrying a weapon. The author asks the question:

> "Police leaders need to keep abreast of the changing landscape of firearm carry laws and ensure that their officers are also kept up to date and trained accordingly. Has agency policy been reviewed with an eye toward all the recent changes on gun laws? Does the agency still allow stops just because someone may be carrying a gun? Perhaps more important, has training included how officers should react when they do encounter someone carrying a gun which becomes more likely every day?"

With the welter of changes in the laws allowing persons to carry a weapon, the department's updated policy and this task might be added to the HR/CT list for a limited period of time.

Conclusion

The HR/CT approach asks police to select the most challenging calls-for-service, pare them down to a manageable number (usually twelve) and put extensive efforts into making their policies as complete and comprehensive enough to provide the essential direction and procedures, in addition providing some quality training documented with lesson plans, and attendance records, and finally developing supervisory personnel through a number of scenario-based training situations, Finally, more extensive training focusing on supervisory excellence should be added.

Require extra review of all of these incidents. Keep some form of statistics on the officers' responses, and when gaps are discovered or improvements needed document your provision of these changes.

CHAPTER 6

SUCCESSFUL PERFORMANCE IN THE HIGH RISK/CRITICAL TASKS

"The focus of every complaint, claim, or lawsuit is an allegation that police performance was short of professional or legal standards."
-Gallagher's Principles #19

"To train not only the expert but the person of responsibility. The aim of training is to do better that which we already do well."
- Zen Proverb

There is nothing more important than having officers achieve the highest level of performance when involved in the High Risk/Critical Tasks (HR/CTs). Why? Those tasks generate about 90-95% of the operational suits based on officers' performance. For the most part these are the targets of the plaintiffs' attorneys' attention. It just makes solid sense that if these tasks are the targets, law enforcement executives and managers must take every precaution to guarantee that when carrying out every aspect of these tasks officers must not overlook any part of what could be considered the professional standards.

To achieve high level performance it must be acknowledged that if it is to be elevated successfully three phases must be in a supportive posture forming a continuum to produce work that is closer to being liability-proof. These three essential supportive phases are:

1. the proactive phase
2. the active phase
3. the reactive phase

The proactive phase: policies and training

This phase constitutes all the activities and processes that officers are exposed to, **prior** to their being able to perform any tasks related to police work in an official capacity. Initially the **policies** of the department must be comprehensive, current, and constitutional. Based on the principle of foreseeability the chief executive or policymaker must provide administrative guidance for all tasks which the officers are expected to perform. Why? Because these policies are the performance standards of the profession, and to avoid liability it is critical to have them in place.

To strengthen performance in this phase it means that the basic law enforcement **training** program must have knowledgeable instructors, a curriculum sufficiently extended to adequately cover all topics in the Job Task Analysis (JTA), frequent updates and revisions where necessary, testing validity and finally comprehensive examinations. It is understood that training from one police academy to another is uneven. Some are considerably better than others; some exist merely as a matter of convenience rather than for credible quality.

The profession must face the reality that in Basic Law Enforcement Training (BLET) there is a glaring omission: in our current basic training programs there is no place for the teaching of any policies especially on the HR/CTs because there are so many variations in the substance of the policies. We allow every department at their discretion to have its own policies unless it is a proprietary academy for one department and even then true training on the policies is not always a reality. I think that the advisory board or the BLET academy director should agree on the major substance of the policies for the HR/CTs making it mandatory that they be taught in the academy. Furthermore, there should be comprehensive examinations on their contents, not merely the common multiple choice but essay exams requiring the correct application of policies to various scenarios.

Let's examine that point about more uniformity of policies to allow them to be taught in the BLET. For the 12 HR/CT policies, if you did a component analysis of them you would find that 80-90% of the policies would be comparable. We should then teach that 80-90% in the BLET and ground our recruits in those critically important policies.

In our search to create a higher degree of protection, did we ever consider the effects of almost total uniformity in the HR/CT policies? Since they would constitute an articulated professional standard of care for the entire law enforcement community in one state, would that achievement make it so much harder for plaintiffs' attorneys to attack one department by offering up a policy that was different, say from a neighboring department?

If all the chief executives were in agreement on the policy, then standing united as it were, the defense as far as policies go, would be unassailable. If the chiefs and sheriffs were to agree on the uniformity of policies at least for the HR/CTs then plaintiffs' attorneys could not search around for stricter policies. The leadership of the law enforcement community would speak with one voice; it would be taking a strong stand for what is professionalism. To have multiple versions of the standards expressed in different policies is not to operate from a position of strength. But, sad to say, even in states where over the years there has been a concerted effort to provide well-written, comprehensive policies through some state office, agencies have not taken advantage of this resource. In litigation the state's own "model policies" often come into evidence against them.

Learning policies during the Field Training Officer (FTO) program

I don't feel that the cursory "review" of policies during the FTO program is anywhere close to sufficient to assess the actual knowledge of a new officer's familiarity with those policies or with the rest of the manual's policies. It has always puzzled me when reviewing FTO daily evaluations as to whether the category for "knowing policies" means policies in general or policies implicated only during the day's patrol activities. When querying FTOs I have never gotten a clear answer even from FTOs in the same department. If that notation evaluates the new officer on policies relating to that day's activities, it is incontrovertible that there are some tasks that the FTO and the new officer were never called upon to handle, for example say civil assistance. If that process is the one that stands for training in the policies, then certain HR/CT policies may never be covered even in this inadequate manner.

If we believe that the plaintiff's side will focus on the HR/CTs because they have the greatest possibilities of winning their case and because they are "critical" tasks, and in their eyes the chances of injury or damages to their client are more prevalent, then our only response must be to make sure all of our officers know the operational procedures associated with those tasks.

Taking the list of the HR/CTs policies how many of them are actually <u>taught</u> to our officers? Does the training go into the accompanying procedures? Or do most of our officers learn all those procedures from their experiences on the street watching other officers?

What about incorporating the 12 HR/CT policy list into the FTO's daily evaluation form? Then the FTO would check off if one of those policies was involved in the day's activities. In this way it would become apparent if a new officer went through the entire FTO period without encountering the pursuit policy, or the domestic violence policy. Of course if all officers were required to <u>know</u> the HR/CT policies and the daily evaluations tracked on whether or not they had actually encountered these activities, then we might be putting them on a better base.

Bridging the transition between the proactive and active phases

I have wondered for a long time why if we believe in the efficacy of the Field Training Officer program, that is having an experienced and specially trained officer paired with a recent academy graduate for a period of close to ten or twelve weeks with daily, weekly and monthly evaluations, why a modified program is not established for new supervisors? I would call it quite uncreatively Field Supervisor's Training program (FST). With checklists and some training material the new first line supervisor would be better versed in the correct manner of performing many of the tasks which might be quite new.

The active phase: supervision

Our first line supervisors (FLS) labor under a series of heavy restrictions. They are as follows:

1. a lack of real support from the second level of supervision – and probably up the line
2. an absence of real adequate, relevant training
3. training if comes, is usually after the assumption of supervisory responsibilities

4. the inadequate training they have been exposed to as officers themselves, - principally because their supervisors were inadequately prepared.
5. the unique role first line supervisors have in the organization since they are the only ones standing with a foot in two worlds: the operational one and the extension of the management world

Are all appointments to supervisory positions permanent? Or can they be made probationary with the judgment that some are not ready to assume the supervisory mantle? Should we have the appointees prove to a certain degree that they are ready to handle all the responsibilities of this critical position?

Lack of support

It has been my observation that even when supervisors experience good training, and moreover they have the will and desire to be better supervisors, they get mediocre support, particularly from the second level of supervision, usually lieutenants. The lieutenants are also a product of little, timely management training. They do not see that it is their responsibility to nurture better methods of supervision from those supervisors that they are overseeing.

I feel that one of the greatest gaps in our defenses akin to that of the first-line supervisors is the failure to prepare our second level and to require them as a number one priority to work with the first level, for in developing them to be better supervisors there would be an appreciable effect on the service delivery.

When first line supervisors strive to do better, to work as much as possible individually with their subordinates, we observe because of the lack of support and encouragement, their enthusiasm tapering off and petering out. We then have lost the benefits of the training.

Inadequacy of training

It is unacceptable to think that two or three days or even a week of supervisory training will counter the skimpiness of the prior preparatory efforts. Those few days will not embed the best principles in the participants, and that is if the training is the best in the profession. Much of that training is not broad enough, and does not get the best habits into long term memory. Finally it is not practical and realistic enough to be directly relevant to the street.

I have often tried this exercise with first line supervisors. Divide the participants into groups of seven or eight, and give each group a specific challenging task that a first line supervisor might be called upon to handle. These topics might be: an officer involved shooting, a case of child abuse, domestic abuse by a police officer, or a barricaded subject. Here is the assignment: list the specific tasks which you would expect the first arriving supervisor to perform in the initial twenty minutes on the scene.

Groups working on the different topics are always able to create a list of ten to fifteen tasks. After a quarter of an hour, the groups would switch topics and lists. They are now asked to add tasks to the list started by another group which they invariably do.

I then make some observations after asking this question: "Is the list complete? Are these all the tasks which we expect of the first arriving supervisor?" Responses are usually guarded: "Well, almost all" or "Just about all" or "Pretty much everything." There has never been a group that has definitively voiced the opinion that the list is complete, if the supervisor did all that was on their list, we could not expect anything more.

Now some of my observations: if a group of supervisors working for a quarter of an hour makes a list in the comparative quiet of the training environment, and then has a second group augment its list, and yet we acknowledge that it is not complete, what happens when under stressful conditions one supervisor faces that type of demanding incident?

To assist first line supervisors in these challenging situations I developed a **<u>Supervisor's Field Manual Checklist</u>** which enumerated twenty odd types of incidents, and compiled every suggested task that could be performed. The **Manual** we said could be displayed on the hood of a car and the supervisor would go down the list making certain that all the tasks were taken care of. We recommended that supervisors could make notes when the opportunity arose on the checklist sheet itself to facilitate a subsequent report.

This was in the days of print and hard copies. But if the approach in any way assisted the supervisor in performing at a higher level, or if it made supervisors more confident in their roles, and if it helped them learn more of what to do when confronted with these incidents, then it was worthwhile. I conjecture that the same process could with modern technology be employed today. In summary, it is an approach that becomes ongoing training for supervisors. The notes made at the scene would make reports more complete, and in combination with the checklist could assist in after-action critiques.

The timing of the training

How long is it that supervisors have to wait before they are given any supervisory training? This factor in combination with others makes it even more arduous for success to come out of any training they receive.

Their exposure to supervisory training as officers

The reality is that most officers from the first day on the job are exposed to many supervisors who are inadequately prepared for that position. Then they find themselves promoted to that position. It is incontrovertible that if the supervisory practices and performance which officers are exposed to in a particular department are deficient, or if supervisors have not assumed the various roles of trainer, policy exemplar, quality control inspector, and liability gatekeeper during the new supervisor's years as an officer, and if there is not a strong leadership model exposed to them, then the new supervisors will naturally supervise in the manner that they had been supervised. A one-week training program possibly made available only after many months or even years in that position will prove highly ineffective. But we blithely check off supervisor' training while hoping for extraordinary results.

The unique role of first-line supervisors

First line supervisors are unique because they are the only ones in any organization that stand with a foot in two worlds. One world is where services are delivered, most tasks are performed and where any incidents which later lead to lawsuits are played out. The other foot is delicately stretched out to the world of management since for any executive, any manager to achieve any goal or objective they must realize that they need the cooperation and assistance of the first line supervisor.

It can be said that the reach and the effectiveness of the department's executive to affect the operational level is based on the effectiveness of the first level of supervision. If the supervision is not of high quality, then tasks will not get done at the level that assures management of better chances to avoid liability.

Management must realize the quandary that first line supervisors are placed in and provide better training pre- and post-promotion. It must be observed unless this peculiar stance of the first line supervisor is recognized, that it is perfectly natural for supervisors to favor the operational world with whom they are most familiar. The consequence of this leaning is that the expectations of management for the supervisor to be supportive of the management agenda is not fulfilled. We pay a price for that omission, and chiefs' jobs are made proportionally more difficult.

The reactive phase

In the Reactive Phase we look at performance that has been completed. This phase is characterized by the following:

1. performance evaluations
2. audits
3. inspections
4. commendations
5. remedial actions
6. discipline

Performance evaluations

While it seems natural that there should be some review of individual performance, there are many departments that don't have any. In some departments these evaluations are prohibited by the collective bargaining agreement. Yes, in other departments they are performed but the results are not accurate or truly indicative of actual performance.

There is always a constant search for the perfect evaluation form and while that might be commendable, I know that there are two problems associated with the faulty perceptions conveyed by the performance evaluations. These problems are:

a. the absence of any preparation or training in how to complete a more accurate evaluation.
b. the lack of a systemic process for gathering information on performance on a regular basis. The technology exists to provide ready access to recordkeeping that can capture on a daily basis information on performance. It often happens that incidents involving officers that happen in close proximity to the evaluation being filled out, skew the gradations one way or another.
c. the failure on the part of many supervisors to observe enough performance of officers to make accurate judgments.
d. because supervisors cannot sufficiently document and justify performance especially that which is marginal or below standards, evaluations are raised to the point where the evaluator feels there will be little chance of a challenge.

Gathering data can best be accomplished by observing actual performance. Too often supervisors by reason of requirements made by management, spend all or too much of their duty time bound to the office for various forms of paperwork. Some, in spite of the paperwork get out, on the streets more frequently and others only occasionally.

I feel that evaluations are important enough that a FLS should on occasion even ride with his officers to get a better feel for their style and to observe how the officers handle themselves in different types of calls-for-service.

When it comes to supervising, it is necessary for there to be a supportive style present, one that is ready to commend good performance, to distinguish it and have it stand out from performance that is just ordinary.

If supervisors' *modus operandi* is such that in reading reports and observing performance, they habitually comment to officers that the "incident could not have been handled any better," or that "it was right in line with the policy and procedures," the FLS, in turn, conveys to the officers that the supervisors know what the officers' best performance levels are.

If there comes a time when the officer's performance is below standards, in talking with the officer, the opening question to the officer might be: "Officer Jones, was the manner in which you handled that call your best performance?" But if the relationship has been established that the FLS has repeatedly commented on good performance, on this occasion the officer might respond with: "No, I could have done it better." In that manner there is more chance for the interchange to be productive, because the officer could have explained how he or she might have done it better, imprinting more indelibly the correct procedure.

For the FLS who only calls in the officers when there is something wrong, the officers' natural reaction is for them to obstinately dig in their heels and try to defend themselves. However, if the supportive stance of the FLS is evident from previous exchanges, if the officer knows that the FLS has recognized good performance and in one meeting out of ten, now questions the quality of how the incident was handled, there is a different dynamic present, more productive of improvement and a more constant and higher level of performance.

Audits and inspections

I believe that performance should be reviewed to guarantee that units or working groups or individuals are constantly getting better at whatever they are doing. Audits and inspections directed not toward individuals, but toward these working groups are processes that could apply here. I see these two processes as focused on finding out how well our personnel are performing, of discerning any means of improving that performance, and finally of providing a measuring point to gauge future progress. The audit could look at all the activities of a division or unit or it could possibly with external assistance look at every aspect of a department. It is of particular value when the agency has undergone some form of organizational trauma, such as a major verdict in a lawsuit going against the department. In its agency-wide application it could be conducted just prior to or immediately after the nomination of a new chief executive.

There was a time when law enforcement agencies more regularly conducted inspections usually through a specially designated section or unit. The inspection might focus on patrol, or just traffic stops or DUI stops.

Either one of these processes should search for every factor that might improve performance of the unit. The composition of the audit or inspection team should be familiar enough with a fairly wide range of components to suggest improvements in policy, training, and supervision. It should look at data where available, analyze the data, and make recommendations based on their interpretations of the data.

Commendations

I have met agency heads that refuse to issue any form of commendations giving the reason that "the officers are only doing what they are paid to do." My retort would be to this chief: "If that is true, when you find someone not doing the job or doing it incorrectly, do you take money from their salaries?"

Obviously they did not. If commendations make it in any way easier to do better, why not employ them. Commendations, however, issued too frequently or for less than serious reasons tend to debase the effect of the commendations. I came across one chief of a 240 member department who when a local service club contacted him so that they could commend "an officer of the year," his only nomination was an officer who had saved a cat from a fire in an apartment. Was there nothing of greater significance done by those 240 officers than saving a cat? Commendations not issued in a timely manner become less effective and appreciated. Today there exist computer programs that will quickly capture a commendation, send copies to supervisors and to the individual named. This is not in any way replacing personal exchanges with some formal documentation.

Commendations can be merely verbalized, or can be part of a FLS's style and can show that the FLS is interested, is observing performance (as in the FLS saying to the officer: "I read your last report and it was very complete and well done"), and that he/she cares.

Remedial actions

When an officer's performance has fallen short of the standards and is not in conformity with the policies and procedures, it is a proven protection for the department and for the supervisor for some form of remediation to be recommended and better still carried out. The remediation might be additional training, reviewing a particular policy, reviewing some form of computer-based training, or attendance at a special class. The remediation must be documented.

Too often there is remediation recommended at one level with no follow up; or there is a recommendation with no available avenue for remediation as in "the officer should get more pursuit driver training" when there is no track or facility where it could be accomplished. Obviously remediation can only be used once or twice with one individual and in the normal pattern of progressive correction with subsequent violations there must be more consideration of discipline of a more formal type.

Discipline

For serious failure to perform according to standards and policies, the FLS might be allowed to recommend the suspension of any officer for one to three days. After an Internal Affairs investigation a recommendation might proceed to the chief executive for a formal suspension of longer duration. However, the discipline should have a justifiable consistency, depending on the circumstances and duration.

Discipline and Internal Affairs frequently are signs of a system failure, because they are only present when the other activities and phases have somehow not achieved the desired results. Ideally they would generally be present since the early phases: the proactive and another active were performed so well that there was no need for corrective action. We are a long way from that state.

Conclusion

Performance cannot be improved or raised to a higher level unless all phases of the performance continuum are employed. The proactive and active phases are mandatory in their entirety, and it is hoped that the reactive phase can be present in evaluations, audits and inspections to increase quality and frequency with a reduction in the need for discipline.

CHAPTER 7

THE MEANING OF AN OATH

"But I have promises to keep, and miles to go before I sleep, and miles to go before I sleep."
                                                            -Robert Frost

"No country can subsist a twelvemonth where an oath is not thought binding, for the want of it must necessarily dissolve society."
                                                            -William Murray

"Integrity is the fixed disposition, the firm resolve to do the right thing when there is no one there to make sure we do it."
                                        -<u>Cops and Character</u> by Edwin deLattre

The foundation of our society rests upon the durability of oaths. There is something sacred in an oath. As Lance Morrow said in a 1981 **Time** magazine article commenting on the air controllers' strike during President Reagan's early years: "But promises, contracts and oaths are the acts of will and intelligence and anticipation that make a society coherent, that hold it together. If they cannot be trusted, then the whole structure begins to wobble."

For people who have important positions, people to whom we should look up and people we expect more of and hold to a higher standard, we ask them to make a solemn promise, an oath to uphold the laws, abide by certain values and rules, and perform their work with a transcendent quality. We ask our elected and appointed public officials to swear oaths; the same is true for our doctors, our judges, and our new citizens, and we try and stabilize marriage by the pronouncement of vows, certainly a form of oath. Realizing the powers and authority vested in our police officers, we require them to swear an oath.

The foundation of an officer's values and beliefs must be the sanctity of the oath of office for it is there that the officer swears to uphold the Constitution and the laws of the state. Officers voluntarily assume immense responsibilities and broad authority unmatched in our society. It is that power and authority given to them by the government to enforce laws, restrict a person's freedom, use legitimate and appropriate force, and to serve and protect that community.

The act of oathtaking transforms and elevates a citizen to a position of respect which the oathtaker is required to earn. It is not the completion of the academy that merits this respect; the academy prepares a recruit to take the oath. How well are those recruits prepared to do that, if at all? The oath allows the person to put on the uniform and to carry the accoutrements of this new position. Having the mantle of this unique authority draped on the officer's shoulders, all who move to this place, who stand elevated among others, must accept the concomitant burden of accountability and the higher standards even the courts acknowledge.

Unfortunately in our society we learn of people who violate their oaths; judges who accept bribes, politicians who curry illegal favors, and officers who indulge in a surprisingly wide range of misconduct. I hope we can remain shocked by this form of ethical cowardice, and not, because of its frequency, become inured to its disclosure.

We entrust these powers and this authority in most cases to fairly young individuals in their mid-twenties whose personal value systems are still in the formative stages. We ask them to raise their right hands and to repeat the solemn words of the oath of office, and then their lives are changed. They carry the badge and with it the concomitant power to keep our communities safe.

These powers and this unique authority are given to our police officers after the completion of Basic Law Enforcement Training (BLET) of for 800 to 1000 hours. This curriculum contains a myriad of sessions given to skill development (self-defense), knowledge of hundreds of laws, various procedures and a good deal of physical fitness.

Upon reviewing the BLET curricula of various police academies around the country, of inquiring of persons conversant with the contents of police training, I have yet to find any police training academy that spends any time on the meaning and implications of the oath of office. I mean even a two-hour block of solid instruction.

(Full disclosure: as Director of Criminal Justice Standards and Training for the state of Florida in the early 1980s, responsible for supervising the curriculum in the state's 45 police training establishments and their curricula, it never crossed my mind to include training on the meaning of an oath as an essential part of the recruits' preparation for policing.)

The oath of office is the foundation of the entire value system which we then presume is present in all of our police officers. Usually the graduating trainees are administered the oath upon graduation from the proprietary academy or by the chief of the department or mayor of the jurisdiction where they will spend their careers. I have never found there to be any explanation given to these officers about what it means to make an oath, or no real training to explain the magnitude of the authority and burden bestowed on them.

The officers will swear many other oaths in their careers, from their appearances in court, and to depositions in civil proceedings. If they have no real grasp of what it means to swear an oath from their academy days, how seriously might they take swearing oaths in court and those for depositions?

I propose that it become mandatory that all police academies have, (just prior to the completion of the academy and the subsequent swearing-in ceremony), their graduates apprised directly of the obligations they freely are taking upon themselves and the expectations that society has of them. It would be a reminder of the obligation to uphold the constitution, and to not deprive any person of their rights. Even the stated values of the department to which they are swearing this allegiance could be included. I would further suggest that each graduate be called to the front, to pronounce his or her oath individually facing the gathering of parents, friends and soon-to-be fellow officers.

Think of how many police departments who have stated values list "integrity." The mark of one who is upholding that value is one who is upholding the oath of office. But the oath taken with full meaning and acquiescence of the individual trainee can infuse and stabilize the department's values, adding much to making them truly living values in all of the officer's actions, They themselves would shine daily, standing as much needed exemplars for all citizens.

In preparing training on the development of corporate values for law enforcement agencies I was struck by the oath that seventeen-year old Athenian youths in 500 B.C. swore to their city. It goes as follows:

> "We will never bring disgrace on this our city by an act of dishonesty or cowardice. We will fight for the ideals and sacred things of the city both alone and with many. We will revere and obey the city's laws and will do our best to incite a like reverence and respect in those above us who are prone to annul them or set them at naught. We will strive increasingly to quicken the public's sense of civic duty. Thus in all these ways we will transmit this city, not only not less, but greater and more beautiful than it was transmitted to us."

Could at least the thoughts, if not the actual wording of the Athenian oath with the necessary emendations be added to the police oath of office?

We rely on our police to hold together the fragile fabric of our society. The raising of their consciousness to the fullest extent of the obligations which they have voluntarily accepted can only contribute to a higher level of performance, that most desirable of goals.

I find that many departments have adopted values statements, which highlight the three to five values that characterize the mission of the organization. While commendable, this posting of the values in many departments does not affect the manner in which policing is carried on. The statement of the values of the organization has to be a living document, not just something on the wall.

Once when conducting training on values for a rather large metropolitan police department with all of their executives and top level managers present, I listed a few values and asked how much they influenced the participants' conduct? How much did the values elevate the officers' performance? One assistant chief raised his hand and asked why I had selected those particular values. I pointed to the plaque on the wall which boldly proclaimed those values: integrity, service, honor, and fairness, and posited that those were the department's stated values. Someone else chimed in saying that there was one of those plaques in every office in the department. Unconscious of these values, oblivious to their critical place in achieving the department's mission, it seemed they had little or no influence on the way business was conducted.

Some departments provide business cards for all their officers; a smaller number even include an officer's photo. Some on the reverse side list the mission and values of the department. I have suggested, since the card is already personalized with the officer's name photo, that there be a signature space for officers to sign their names after this statement: "I conduct myself according to these values," or something similar.

Values must be part of the fabric of the department. One enlightened executive said his department took close to a year through small group discussions to select their values, and then an additional three years to say the department was value-guided rather than policy-driven. He said that was equivalent to "planting our flag" and then standing and defending it.

Now no department can operate without policies and procedures, but the values can be incorporated into the policies. In that department referenced above, the chief mandated that the values find a place in every policy, in every training session. He reserved an hour or so in every single training session to speak of the values and to show support for their critically important place in every aspect of the department's service. Despite his national role in law enforcement activities, and the demands of a department of that size (1200 officers), he felt it was essential that he invest this time in pushing forward his personal mission of leading the department.

I know that the oath of office appropriately emphasized and linked to the stated values of the organization can be a support for a stronger commitment to the highest level of performance and integrity.

Our society needs dedicated persons who will strive to better the conditions in our communities, and not just maintain them at current levels, or stand by as they sink even lower. Many, many officers are involved in the communities in which they live and serve; they remain conscious of the inherent power in their positions to be role models. We need every officer to do that.

A renewed emphasis on the meaning of an oath coupled with the continuous re-stating of a department's values into every aspect of its administration will undoubtedly accomplish much to maintain every member's commitment to doing what is expected, raising performance levels, reducing the burden of liability and passing the Gallagher-Westfall Group's Leadership Test:

"Am I doing:

- The right thing?
- At the right time?
- In the right way?
- For the right reason?"

CHAPTER 8

SUPERVISION: QUALITY CONTROL FOR PERFORMANCE

"No factor is more important to avoid liability and raise performance than the quality of supervision, especially at the first level."
-Gallagher Principle #7

"Most catastrophic judgments result from ignoring the fundamentals over which we should have control as chiefs, managers and supervisors."
-Gallagher Principle #17

Executives constantly bemoan the quality of first line supervision (FLS) at the sergeant's level, indicating that it is their most pressing internal problem. However, if that is true, one might expect them individually and as a group to take dramatic measures to improve the performance of these supervisors, and lavish attention, resources and support on helping them perform the job at the maximum level. It is not totally understood that the easiest way to make the positions of upper level management easier, is to have first line supervisors performing at their optimum levels. The response is nowhere close to what it should be once you appreciate their importance to the quality of policing and the goal of the decrease of liability.

The word "supervision" comes from two Latin roots: *supra* or "over," and *visus* to "see" combining to mean "to look over." It does not mean to "overlook." We have already mentioned something about the problems of supervisors standing with a foot in two worlds, that of the officer at the operational level and that of an extension of management. It is that particular positioning that makes the FLS so critically important to the quality of police services.

Let's take that thought a little further. I say that it becomes nearly impossible for department executives and top level managers to forge change and to have policies properly become operational without excellent first line supervision. We have heard how those supervisors are uniquely unprepared for this demanding role in the sense that a week or two of supervisory training are inadequate. There are many excellent first line supervisors in policing; somehow they have managed to mature professionally into models of what is required. But their number has to increase to the point where they become the rule rather than the exception. Finally it is almost universal that few supervisors are actually trained for this role before they are thrust, it might be said *in medias res,* or right into the middle of things.

Supervision must be supportive of the officers, and supportive of good and high level performance. The essence of the role is to assist officers in becoming the very best that they can be, and to counsel them when necessary when they are falling short of standards. Supervisors must accept and develop a proficiency in a number of roles, especially after they have been trained in the best manner of exercising them.

I see first level supervisors as exercising six different roles which are:

1. liability gatekeepers
2. quality control inspectors
3. standards and policies exemplars
4. trainers
5. monitors
6. counselors

1. Liability gatekeepers

This role places a critical burden on the shoulders of the first line supervisors as the ability of the chief executive to reach the operational level is only possible through the supervisors. Without good supervision the mission, the corporate values, the goals and objectives of the department, and the best policies and training amount to little because they will remain detached from the actual performance in the street.

It is a valid assumption that supervisors cannot be present for every incident involving the officers serving under them, but good supervisors exude a sense of control even when not there, enough that their virtual presence by their supervisory style can contribute to the adherence to policies and standards.

As gatekeeper in combination with the supervisors' other roles, they if properly trained and versed in the correct assessment of potential actions that might lead to liability, must take a stand seeing if officers are coming too proximate to complaint- and lawsuit-generating consequences of their actions. True, complaints and lawsuits can be generated when officers do exactly as they have been taught and exactly in conformity to policies. There is no way to avoid some complaints from disgruntled arrestees. The awareness expected of the first line supervisor is to recognize when selected actions are going over the line.

2. Quality control inspectors

We would never purchase a car from a company that bragged that its cars were less expensive because they had eliminated the whole inspection function on the production line. There are vehicular lemons turned out even with inspectors.

Inspectors watching over the flow of police activities and the subsequent reporting on those activities must - with the policies and standards in mind - reject anything that is not truly quality performance. Even if the incident itself cannot be affected, the reporting of all incidents can be brought to a higher standard.

The quality control inspector will not hesitate to reject reports that are not complete, do not adequately cover the requirements of the incident and while adhering to the truth do not present the officers' actions in the strongest possible manner. The supervisors' comments or counseling in accepting their supervisory responsibilities and making their thoughts known to officers have to be couched in terms of helping and supporting the officer in performing better and better, but not done in a critical, blaming way.

To fail to do this allows performance to slip to lower levels and can create a downward spiral in quality. One supervisor remarked to me: "You can't expect me to read all of those reports, do you?" Well, actually yes, I do because in signing them without applying a discerning eye, implies ratification of those actions, some of which might be violations of policy or even something further, constitutional violations. Good supervisors, at once well trained and supported by those above them, can affect dramatic changes for the better.

3. Standards and policies exemplars

If there is anyone who exemplifies the values, standards and policies of the department it must be the first line supervisor. At some point the policies and values must take life and the first line supervisor must be a vitally alive model of what is expected of someone who has been around the department for a number of years, someone totally imbued with the core values characterizing all actions, and ensuring they are performed within the parameters of the department's guidance. Let people read the values and policies in the first line supervisor's attitude toward performing all of their duties.

They must know the policies, be able to respond to questions about proper procedures, show by their actions how tasks are to be performed, and correct those officers whose performance falls short of the standards.

4. Trainers

Capitalizing on the first line supervisor's experience in handling the full range of incidents, their very actions become a lesson for those less experienced in some duties. Conscious of this role, the FLS will patiently explain methods to those who are less experienced, will point out to others how they could do the task better, and what they might do to improve. This role would have the FLS actually sitting down with some officers, going over a procedure, and reminding them of a policy, perhaps giving them an article that explains the proper approach at length. Finally, aware of what training might be occurring in a more formal setting, the supervisor might recommend that the officer be assigned to those sessions. However, formal training might be some distance off in the future, but that is not to be a substitute for some informal training delivered more immediately by the FLS. These actions must always be documented in a supervisor's notebook for this might easily refute the omnipresent complaint about negligent supervision embedded in so many lawsuits.

5. Monitors

To be effective, the FLS cannot be tied to a desk, or see their prime responsibility limited to being so immersed in paperwork that there is no street presence. To burden the FLS with this work is counterproductive, for there will be a multiplicity of problems emanating from that unit resulting from the absence of the experienced eye of the FLS on the street. Monitoring requires pointing out where any performance falls short of standards or is contrary to policies. Officers who find some difficulty in complying should be the subject of additional "backup" on calls to see them providing the service.

The function of monitoring consists of observing and checking up on performance. Since supervisors frequently are the ones given the responsibility of formally evaluating the officers, monitoring could naturally require the supervisor to conduct ridealongs with all of the officers and back them up with a similar purpose. The report filed after an incident may not include certain signs or evidence of a heavy-handedness, a brusque demeanor, or rude comments from the officer. This is the venue to observe an officer's infinite patience, a certain compassion for a victim, or a brief and timely explanation for the officer's actions. Reports don't reveal these important points.

6. Counselors

The FLS must be aware of certain signs that an officer may not be performing at their recognized level of competence. The FLS must look for signs there are other pressures impinging on the officer: a failing marriage, financial worries, an incipient drug or alcohol problem, or the inability to get along with the other members of the squad. While officers may not welcome any personal questions, where the personal problems touch upon performance or the quality of interaction with others, the FLS may be obliged to step in at least temporarily.

However, the supervisor whose style is abrupt and seemingly uncaring, cannot exhibit this caring side on a given day. The treatment of the officers over time by the FLS if sensitive and apparently showing an interest in all the officers may establish a better basis for a franker discussion when certain signs surface.

Taking the function of counselor, the supervisor will when appropriate take officers aside to not only point out deficiencies but also to constantly recognize and commend them when they do work that stands out for their correct adherence to accepted procedures and policies in trying situations.

Good supervisors will call in officers to tell them how pleased they are with an officer's superior performance saying: "I know you can do this job and can do it well. You've just shown me that you can." If at some time, an officer's conduct falls short of standards, and if a supervisor has called someone in nine times to recognize that officer, the tenth time the question to be posed is: "Was the way you handled this call the best you can do? Does this represent your best performance?"

If the officer knows the supervisor is interested enough to recognize good performance, the officer's response could be: "You're right, Sarge, I could have done it better. This is what I should have done." Commonly when officers are called in solely when something is wrong, and the interactions are mostly negative, it is natural for them to be defensive and to dig in his/her heels. With a more supportive style of supervision, the officer is more open to a candid assessment and a realization that supervisors know through past performance they could have done better. Then the door is open to real improvement.

Improving the quality of first line supervision

To improve the quality of preparation and performance of first-level supervisors some of the recommended steps are quite obvious:

1. Improve the quality of supervisory training prior to the assumption of supervisor's responsibilities.
2. Consider the initiation of a Supervisor's Field Training program. If the Field Training Program for officers has proven its efficacy over the years, then there is a crying need for a similar type program for supervisors, but certainly not of the same duration. In any department at least one excellent supervisor can be identified. Then a

one- or two-week program must be initiated for the two supervisors, the veteran and the newly-minted supervisor to work together going over the major tasks and providing support in those early days. A good suggestion is to develop checklists or an abbreviated Job Task Analysis. The probability of a positive return over time and the initiation of a new supervisory culture are worth the time and effort.

3. Lieutenants for the most part supervise sergeants and in this capacity they should have responsibility for the performance of the first-level supervisor. While executives might question their doings and criticize the mediocre performance of first line supervisors, they seldom if ever task the lieutenants at the second level with improving the lot of their subordinates. We hold the sergeant responsible for the officers. Why not place more onus on the lieutenant for the quality of their subordinates? How can lieutenants receive good evaluations if they have poor performing subordinates, e.g. the sergeants?
4. Make sure that lieutenants support the valiant efforts of the first-level to improve by working with them in a cooperative mode.

The 3 R and 3S Process

With the best of supervisory environments there may come a time when corrective action, reprimands, or discipline have to take place. What follows is a template to understand better the dynamics present in this process.

	3Rs	**3Ss**
Step 1	**REPRIMAND**	purpose: to **STOP** the improper conduct
Step 2	**RETRAINING** **REDIRECTION** **REMEDIATION**	purpose: to **START** the desired conduct
Step 3	**RECOGNITION**	purpose: to **SUPPORT/SUSTAIN** the new conduct

When a reprimand is given, or discipline is imposed, it is an acknowledgement that a person's conduct is not up to standards, that performance is below or contrary to the stated standards, that work habits are sloppy, or for any number of other reasons. The purpose of the action is to get the officer to cease doing what is not acceptable. However, standing alone very often the reprimand can have some negative results in the manner in which it is administered, or received. To the persons reprimanded this action might only serve to have them be of a mind to not change conduct, or to see the process as directed personally at them rather than at the conduct which was at fault. Compliance might be grudgingly developed if only to get the supervisors off the officers' backs.

To accompany the reprimand, it is necessary to do everything possible to exhibit the acceptable conduct, or to offer the person some assistance with incorporating the proper conduct into their performance, or to start the process of change.

Finally give the reprimanded officer the chance to come back, to recognize and support the efforts at the acceptable conduct over time. The supervisor must take the time and make the effort to sustain the change in conduct.

Who will watch the watchers?

From my perspective one of the greatest causes of the ineffectiveness of FLS is the failure to train and assign the proper supervisory responsibilities to the second level of supervision, the lieutenants. I have seldom heard about any attention being brought on that rank for the alleged inadequacies of the FLS, nor have I heard about clearly outlined responsibilities for the support and for the fostering of improvement by the FLS.

Lieutenants must be charged with actively supervising the FLS and to work with them to improve their skills and the proper oversight over their squads. When lieutenants are told that this requirement is their most important duty and are held to it, the FLS may get more of the assistance they need. If this is not done, the FLS will continue to be a prominent weakness in the whole liability protection process.

Supervision as service

In surveys in the United States and Britain, police say the greatest stressor on the job, is management and supervision, both internal stressors. The officers acknowledge that the manner in which they are managed and supervised causes them the greatest stress.

If supervision and management were to assume the responsibility of serving those under them, this major cause of discomfiture and dislike of the job might dissolve. If there is more of a commitment to the internal community with a lessening of stress, those officers might display a better frame of mind to show that protection and service to the external community.

If supervision and management are devoid of the attitude of service, it is a magnified challenge for officers to show those positive acts to the people with whom they meet in the course of their daily interactions. With a more positive slant to the styles of supervision, officers may be more apt to avoid some of the actions that might generate complaints and potential lawsuits.

There is no magic cure for liability; only a combination of various efforts in which each contributes something to the push for a reduction that will eventually accomplish a lessening of liability's pressure. Policies, better and more training, supervision and discipline and even commendations must be considered as only being effective so far. We cannot overlook the contribution of better supervisory and management styles, an improved organizational climate, and the effort to do anything that makes it easier for all to perform at a higher level.

CHAPTER 9

VIEWING THE POLICE FROM THE OTHER SIDE

"Like the dinosaur he had power without the ability to change, and strength without the capacity to learn."

-Rollo May

"To win in the liability arena you have to understand and think like the opposition."

-Gallagher's Principles #3

We have seen something about the Plaintiff's Five Points of Attack in the third chapter, "The Opposition's Game Plan." Just a reminder: the First Point focuses on the <u>officer</u> and all the details of the incident. The next four points concentrate not on the officer but on the <u>department.</u> These four targets are: policy, training, supervision, and finally discipline and corrective action.

It is essential to have a triggering incident, an interaction between police and some members of the public. Once the plaintiff's attorney has the incident, then the complaint and subsequent federal or state civil actions include almost by routine charges of negligence in direction, training and supervision.

These charges, though, are not usually supported by a concentrated effort over the run-up through the production of documents, their expert's reports, and depositions. To further the development of their cases I predict that plaintiffs' attorneys will learn to be more aggressive in pursuing and buttressing their cases in these areas. One striking example in the last few years has been their progress in examining the internal affairs process and officers' records when they get them trying to show by the analysis of statistics and data that there is some form of custom or practice of constitutional violations.

If we truly want to progress in our mounting of better defenses we have to closely observe what these attorneys are doing and understand our fragile capabilities in some critical areas. To this end, this chapter will feature the development of a plaintiff's case. We will stand by plaintiff's attorneys and be the police expert whom they will rely on to build the case.

Your assignment, if you chose to accept, will be to use the summary of the incident, and then the framework of the Plaintiff's Five Points of Attack to build up a list of documents, records and studies that you, the plaintiff's expert, would need to fashion your report. Secondly, you are to lay out the basis for the civil rights complaint against the police agency citing resources, programs and critical policies and accompanying training. Finally summarize your opinions.

Summary of the Case

Directions: You as an <u>expert for the plaintiff</u> have been asked to apply the Plaintiff's Five Points of Attack. Some starter questions:

1. What documents would you request through discovery? List them.
2. What administrative guidance would you expect the department to have? Name the policies.
3. What training would you expect the deputies to have? Basic and in-service?
4. What resources would you expect the deputies to be able to call upon, what should they have at their disposal to handle the incident?
5. What initial considerations should have guided their actions?
6. What actions would professional standards dictate for the deputies' response?
7. What are the alternative approaches which could/should have been used?
8. Was the use of the taser justifiable?
9. Was the use of deadly force justifiable?
10. What complaints would you recommend filing for the lawsuit?
11. What opinions would you offer?

The Facts:

Shortly before 11 p.m. on the evening of June 29, 2008 Michael Gordon, (a twenty-seven year old) on his way home, received a call from his mother, Jerri Gordon, asking Michael to get to the house as soon as possible. There was trouble with his father. Upon arriving home, he called 911, telling the operator (1) his father was depressed, (2) was talking of suicide, and (3) his father had a neighbor's gun.

At that time, Michael's father, David Gordon, was in the backyard of his house talking to his wife, Jerri, and their neighbor, Thomas Cartwright.

Michael Gordon made it clear to the operator that his father was (1) not a threat to anyone but himself, (2) things would probably be resolved calmly among his father, mother and the neighbor (3) his father was taking a number of medications and (4) he was currently seeing a psychiatrist. These points were relayed to the responding deputies.

Shortly after, four sheriff's deputies from the 200- member department, arrived in the area, taking care to attempt a silent approach even though Michael Gordon and those in the back yard were able to hear the sirens off in the distance. The deputies were supervised by Sgt. Putman.

Michael Gordon, still in the driveway of the neighbor's house spoke to the sheriff's contingent telling the deputies that his father was calm and not a threat to others.

The Response:

The sergeant immediately starting directing his team: two deputies were assigned deadly force use and two the tasers, indicating that all of them would go into the back yard together. The sergeant told one deputy: "You and I would use the tasers on the subject as soon as we see him."

The Gordon house faced south with the deck and cinder block wall on the north side in the back yard. Along the east and west sides of the back yard of the house were seven-foot high wooden fences, with a 6' wide door on the wooden fence connecting the east side of the house itself to the wooden fence running down the two sides of the back yard extending 100 feet to the northern boundary of the property.

As the group of deputies prepared for their next move, Michael Gordon proposed opening the garage door so that someone could enter through the house, since the front door was locked. From this point a deputy could go downstairs to the basement door opening on the back yard a scant 12' from the location of David Gordon. Michael Gordon stated the sergeant refused to address him, asking only how to get into the back yard.

David Gordon was facing the house or south with his wife, Jerri, standing somewhat to his left a few feet away. Also standing in front of Gordon to the left of Jerri was the neighbor, Thomas Cartwright, The three people had been talking with Gordon for over half an hour since he was "upset and pissed off at life." David Gordon was smoking a cigarette, and had a beer can by his side on the cinder block wall, as he continued the conversation with Jerri and the neighbor.

Sergeant Putman's group rejected the idea of entering through the house, but moved quickly to the right or east side of the building where the door in the wooden fence would allow them to enter the back yard. He formed up his "stack." Putman (he and two other deputies were also on the SWAT team), peeked into the yard to see David Gordon still smoking a cigarette facing the rear of the house.

The sergeant was in the lead position, as the "stack" ran into the backyard, going directly toward Gordon's position on the wall. He immediately tased Gordon while he was still seated on the wall.

Jerri said the (1) deputies made no effort to talk with her husband, (2) that her husband didn't have the gun up for it was behind his back on the wall, and (3) it was only when they charged him that he got up. Thomas Cartwright stated the gun in a holster was "just sitting behind him," that the flashlight in his face and the attempted tasing "scared" Gordon and he got up to move for the door.

Sgt. Putman then ordered one deputy to use his taser, realizing that his first attempt was unsuccessful as David Gordon rose and started moving toward the house, going to the left of the two persons in front of him, while simultaneously his wife, Jerri, backed up quickly so that she was to the left of the basement door close to the house. Thomas Cartwright moved slightly left, or east so that he now occupied the position that Jerri had occupied.

Gordon moved toward the basement door, twelve feet from the wall; he had nothing in his left hand. As was proven by the wounds in his back, he was obviously facing away from the deputies, one of whom situated behind Gordon and slightly to the left of his back, at Sgt. Putman's direction, "Gun! Shoot him!" fired three rounds, all of which struck Gordon in the back fatally wounding him.

David Gordon, who was right handed, had reached a spot close enough to open the handle of the door to the basement, but fell through the doorway. He lay just inside the basement family room with a pool of blood under his chest. The deputies immediately cleared everyone out from the yard, and then without using an evidence bag or taking photos put the gun with blood on its underside into the trunk of the sergeant's car.

Three other deputies responding to the scene, arriving just after the first group of four was moving down the street toward the house. In fact, one radioed Sgt. Putman asking where he wanted them to "set up" but there was no response. Immediately after this, they heard gunshots.

Remember, using the Plaintiff's **Five Points of Attack**, outline your report, assemble your requested list of documents, list your opinions.

1. **First Point:** The Incident Itself

2. **Second Point:** The Policies

3. **Third Point:** Training

4. **Fourth Point:** Supervision

5. **Fifth Point:** Discipline or Corrective Action

Possible Points for Consideration

You might center your attention on the following questions:

1. Did the policies of this sheriff's department meet the national standards and the generally accepted standards for police agencies in a situation like this?
2. Was the training given to the deputies of the sheriff's office under this sheriff adequate and up to national standards in the areas of use of force, critical incident response and dealing with the mentally ill?
3. What was the offense for which the deputies were going to try and arrest Gordon for?
4. Was the employment of the tasers immediately upon entering the yard and even before the subject made any movement a legitimate use of force?
5. Was the use of deadly force against the subject objectively reasonable and justifiable?
6. In the critical policy areas does the department follow its own policies?

Conclusion

After you have outlined your response you might want to turn to Appendix A, and review a complete report on this particular case.

CHAPTER 10

PROFESSIONAL STANDARDS AND THE DYNAMICS OF POLICIES

"Issuing an order is only 10%. The remaining 90% consists in proper and rigorous execution of the order."

-General George C. Patton

"Policy is to be developed and issued in anticipation of the foreseeable field incidents officers can reasonably be expected to encounter. Policy that is subsequent and in reaction to a series of events encountered by officers is more likely to be deficient and is issued in the face of growing organizational pattern of conduct contrary to the substance of the policy."

-Gallagher's Principles # 6

"No law book, no lawyer, no judge can really tell the police officer on the beat how to exercise this discretion perfectly in every one of the thousands of different situations that can arise in the hour-to-hour work of the police officer. Yet we must recognize that we need not choose between no guidelines at all and perfect guidelines. There must be some guidance by way of basic concepts that will assist the officers in these circumstances."

-Chief Justice Warren Burger

A standard is the measure of performance accepted by the police profession. Today in policing when we hear the word "standards" we commonly think of the work of the Commission on Accreditation for Law Enforcement Agencies or CALEA. In its manual the commission lists about four hundred and seventy-five **Standards for Law Enforcement Agencies** which place a clear requirement on the agency calling for the development of a policy, procedure or the standard that might include "an activity, a report, an inspection, equipment or other action," as stated in the CALEA **Manual**.

However, over and above the CALEA standards and the somewhat parallel requirements of the various state accreditation programs, there are other professional or industry standards of care as some would call them. These other standards might be promulgated by the International Association of Chiefs of Police (IACP) or even police professional groups with special areas of focus such as those for police trainers, emergency response teams, hostage negotiators, EVOC instructors, and firearms trainers. While some would say that the statements of these groups are not officially stamped as standards, when it comes to litigation they are quickly invoked by one side or the other as standards, the commonly accepted manner of performing certain tasks or of training officers to perform those tasks. In litigation you will see experts submitting their reports, weighing in on the various aspects of the case.

Mentioning sources of policies I cannot overlook the importance of case law which must, out of necessity, provide direction to anyone formulating policies. As lawsuits are filed and go to court, and the court comes to a decision in many cases there is an appeal. The process could go all the way to the U.S. Supreme Court and any decision emanating from this body becomes in effect a requirement for all police in the country. (At the U.S. Federal District level, that court's decisions exercise the same mandatory requirement for law enforcement agencies in the multi-state district.)

Some years ago the Federal Aviation Administration (FAA) adopted a standard of 100% safe landings and takeoffs. Since I was traveling around the country conducting training sessions and spent a lot of time on planes, I appreciated the standard, as it heightened my safety. Then I got to wondering: if they just adopted that standard of 100% what was the previous standard?

Candidly while I approved the standard I agreed that there probably would be some air plane crashes. But doing some calculating if the standard was slightly less, say 99.9% safe landings and takeoffs, that would mean that one crash in every 1000 takeoffs and landings would be acceptable. Furthermore that would mean one crash daily for the 1000 or so landings and takeoffs at the country's busiest airports, Chicago's O'Hare or Atlanta's Hartfield. Acceptable? Certainly not.

All professions have standards and the standards for police do not place an onerous burden on us if we consider ourselves professionals – which we certainly do. What standards do we expect from our doctors, from our accountants, or from the makers of our new cars? What standard is acceptable for airplane maintenance? Would we accept a 90% standard from our accountant? He or she is certainly correct most of the time. I think that just as much as we expect the highest of standards from these other professionals, that the public whom we serve should anticipate the very same from us. Accepting a very high standard should prompt police to strive harder and harder to achieve it, even if we sometimes fall short. However, if our standard is not the highest, in falling short our performance level is markedly lower.

The welter of professional standards is incorporated into police manuals under the nomenclature of policies, procedures, standard operating procedures (SOPs), directives, rules and regulations. They are then found in training curricula as well. But for the sake of uniformity I will speak of policy, the policy process, and policymakers.

Policies speak of the difference between the right and any possible wrong ways of doing something, or performing a task. They can also assign accountability as in describing the differing roles of the sergeant, the officer and the communications personnel.

To protect and serve

A commonly accepted mission for police is "To protect and serve." This general mission statement generates for me the question of who is to be protected and served. As mentioned previously, the common answer is "the community." Then I ask, "Which one?" I see an internal community and also the external community. Leadership and supervision should be directed ideally toward this bipartite mission in the manner in which persons in these positions carry them out. The better the internal protection and service, the more likely that there will be better protection and service externally

But more to the point, if "to protect and serve" is the general mission of the agency, then we can point to each policy, and say in effect when this police department conducts a pursuit, uses force, arrests someone that policy articulates the particular manner in which the public is protected and served. Taking the pursuit policy for example, its numerous components indicate the number of cars, the use of marked units, a continuous radio commentary, roles and responsibilities of all those involved, what incidents can initiate a pursuit, the balance of the need for apprehension weighed against the risk to the public, the offender and the officers themselves. Police protect and serve when conducting pursuits by observing these policy components. And so on for the other policies.

Two forces and the principle of foreseeability

Two forces are in place forcing the police profession to have policies. They are:

1. the police profession, similar to any other true profession, has a requirement for standards,
2. the courts' demand that there be some form of administrative guidance.

Agency executives become the persons responsible for satisfying the demands of these two forces. They become the "policymakers" to produce the guidance "by reasons of basic concepts that will assist the officer" in doing the right thing in the circumstances related to all the tasks the officer has to perform.

I call this requirement the "principle of foreseeability," in which the policymaker or agency executive is required to issue directions and guidelines for all the tasks which it is envisioned that the officers will be performing. If the task is assigned, there must be the performance standard, or policy for that task put in place. Furthermore, the policies once in place are the conduit to inform the community how they will be "protected and served," and how the range of services will be carried out.

Too often the need for policies is not foreseen; they are issued retroactively in light of some event such as a high speed pursuit ending in fatalities, a barricaded subject incident, or some other event testing the quality of the department's administrative guidance. However, policies issued after the fact rather than before expose the department's vulnerabilities. The officers are missing the needed direction and the plaintiff focuses on this fact. The absence of the needed policies might go under the name of "negligent direction," a form of supervisory negligence.

Therefore the question remains: What are the assigned tasks? What is commonly accepted as the ordinary calls-for-service that the officers will have to respond to? Policy manuals are replete with pages of direction on any number of tasks. But are there some assigned incidents that are quite commonly faced by officers and which are usually not covered by policies?

Policies needed: examples of two commonly assigned tasks

1. Response to teenage drinking parties:

Officers increasingly get calls about loud teenage parties. It is easy to spot the address when the officers see the congestion of the parked cars blocking the street. Neighbors are annoyed because it's late at night, and there is every appearance of drinking inside and outside of the house. When officers arrive they might knock on the door, ask for an adult, direct the partygoers to "quiet it down," and depart with the warning: "If we have to come back, we're going to shut the party down."

Suppose the officers take a stronger stand and decide to shut the party down or return because of a second complaint, and they follow through on their promise. What are the ramifications when officers know there is underage drinking going on, and they take no action but instead warn the partygoers "to keep it down?" The shutting down of the party most likely means that the large group of teenagers, some or all of whom have been drinking, will head to their cars and take off. In their state of varying degrees of intoxication there could be an accident on the way home, and a subsequent lawsuit because they were told in effect by the officers to get on the road which meant getting behind the wheel of a car.

In the absence of a policy on this type of frequently occurring incident, some officers would do as above. Some would try and detain some of the partygoers, some might try to call parents of those they detain; some might enter the house because they can see the overt signs of underage drinking.

Most agencies' officers act without any policy on this topic. (What is your formal policy on this type of incident? I'm sure that in its absence you have a number of informal policies. Your protection as chief comes about when the formal policy, the written one is made operational and stands before the court as your official policy.)

My point is that it is very much a foreseeable task that officers will have to handle and the department's response should have a definite uniformity to it. What must be done is to review state statutes, determine a general policy such as detain as many as possible, call parents, and guide officers as to the circumstances under which they can enter the house. Every part of a procedure for officers should be anticipated and spelled out in the policy; the guidance should be unambiguous. If a number of partygoers cannot be detained and they rush to their cars and escape, the officers' efforts in detaining as many as they can with a clear policy supporting their procedure, should constitute solid protection if one of those fleeing the scene were to get into an accident.

2. Civil assists

Generally it is classified as a "civil assist" when someone, usually a female wants some protection to get her possessions from a house that at one time was shared by her and her partner. In one of my cases, a woman called police saying that she needed to get her daughter's school clothes and her medications from the house which up until recently she had shared with her former boyfriend. Her name was on the lease; she had a key to the house and when told by police that it's a civil matter, she still insisted on going over to the location.

An officer watched while she tried the key in the door unsuccessfully since the male was holding the thumb latch from turning. So the woman climbed over the fence and entered from a back window. Could the officer have stopped her? The next thing the officer heard was the woman screaming: "You gotta a gun! Are you going to shoot me?" The woman's key being left in the lock, the officer entered the property to try to protect the woman. He eventually forced his way in, and shot and killed the man holding the gun which was pointed at the woman.

That's an extreme case. My point is that civil assists of one kind or another do occur, and they might be classified as "low frequency and low criticality" but the officers deserve guidance on the proper procedures and response they should make to these requests. Do they refuse under any circumstances to get involved? Can they stop the person from approaching or entering the property?

The policy process

It brings us to the policy process with the following steps:

1. scanning the environment. What is it that officers are asked to do?
2. reviewing the task, breaking it down into its components
3. determining the department's policy
4. writing/adapting policy in the three part approach: policy statement, definitions, and procedures to be followed
5. then training officers in the policy
6. supervising to make sure that the policy is followed.

Clarification where needed

Sometimes policies appear to be in conflict with one another. For example the pursuit policy might say: "Officers shall not use deadly force against a vehicle" while the deadly force policy says the "officer may use deadly force when in fear of death or serious bodily harm." Example: a car speeds up and heads directly at an officer.

In other examples officers have stated the apparent contradiction when they are told they are "on duty 24/7," they may carry their weapon when off duty, but not if they have been consuming alcoholic beverages. But what action does the officer take if he/she has consumed a few drinks and sees someone being mugged? This is particularly a problem because aside from this guidance in the policies there is absolutely no training, no scenarios presenting situations with guidance as to how the officer should respond. What does "take appropriate action" mean? With no other direction does it mean intervene, act as a witness, or call for uniformed officers?

Questions to be asked

The supposition reigns supreme in law enforcement that once policies are developed and issued that everyone knows them and will follow them. This is a fallacy. Suppose we were to ask every police executive if they knew all the policies in their departmental manual. What is the answer we could expect? How many would answer positively?

I have done this at chiefs' and sheriffs' conferences, asking how many here can stand up and plead guilty to knowing all their own policies and procedures. In one session out of the one hundred and forty agency executives present, not one could admit that he/she knew all their own policies, most of which had their name written across the top.

A follow-up question was asked: "How many policymakers present expect all officers to know all their departmental policies?" Here the answer was unanimous: all of them had that expectation. What's wrong with this situation? Here we have so much of our hopes for high performance based on a principle that it totally flawed. There must be a close re-examination of this process for disseminating the performance standards. Is it possible for an officer to know all the policies?

Objectives of administrative guidance

The administrator of the agency has the responsibility to control the actions of all of its members while providing them guidance to all levels as to how they are to act in the tasks assigned to them. Furthermore, the objectives for this guidance (policies) are to coordinate the agency's efforts in achieving its mission. Another important objective is to be able to hold the personnel of the organization accountable for their performance measured up to the professional standards of conduct laid out in the policies. Law, policy and procedures establish the legal and professional rules of engagement to direct officers' actions.

The policies are written. Now what?

To ensure that policies are known by the officers we must dispel the notion that we can have all the policies known by all the officers. That is impossible.

We have to admit it especially when we contemplate the inadequacy of the training the officers received in those very same policies. If policies are essential for better performance, how do we accomplish the goal of making sure that officers know the policies?

Let's go back to the HR/CTs. The critical importance rests in the performance of these twelve tasks. The better they are performed, the stronger our defenses will be at the points where plaintiffs' attorneys make the biggest efforts to initiate lawsuits.

Some suggestions:

1. in the manual print the HR/CT policies on blue paper
2. establish two categories of policies: "need to know" and "need to reference"
3. annual recertification in all HR/CT policies
4. short videos on HR/CT policies
5. command staff consensus training
6. require that HR/CT policies are an essential part of all training to include the Basic Law Enforcement Training (BLET)
7. employ policies for critiques and reviews of all HR/CT incidents
8. computer assisted training and testing for HR/CT
9. include in commendations and disciplinary actions the relationship of the policy to the incident

1. Blue paper

Place all the HR/CT policies on blue paper to distinguish them from all the others; and/or establish a mini-manual for just those twelve policies. By some means highlight the importance of the HR/CT policies. Have a special section with these policies if they are stored on a computer.

2. Two categories of policies

While some would say all policies are important, that really isn't true. The very existence of the HR/CT policies disproves that. The importance of those twelve or so policies, their focus on the most common liability-generating tasks, and the dire need to bring together an agency-wide attention to these topics require giving them a different status. No officer can know all the policies; it is a myth that executives believe in. Liability protection cannot be built on such a shaky foundation.

My suggestion: Label the twelve HR/CT policies the "need to know" policies. All the others thereby become the "need to reference" policies. That's not to downgrade the importance of all the others, but we have to devise a process where we can guarantee the most important policies are known. All members of the department are at all times held responsible for knowing the "need to know" policies; all personnel are given access to the whole policy manual and it is their responsibility to reference all the other policies, the "need to reference." In a sense the HR/CT policies become a closed book test; the "need to reference" policies are an open book test.

3. Annual recertification

Commonly certain skills require annual recertification, firearms being the most prominent. This certification might be quarterly or semi-annually. In many departments aside from the range there is a classroom session on the policies regarding use of force. That recognizes the fact that for this particular HR/CT that the policy review should accompany the actual training. I say that for all the HR/CTs there should be annual recertification. They are that important. If you are interested in cutting down on potential liability, and if the established custom of having the force policy reviewed on the occasion of regular firearms requalifications, the same benefits might come from the review annually of all HR/CTs. The officers will certainly be asked to perform a number of the other HR/CTs more often than the one relating to deadly force. (Admittedly, however, the use of other levels of force will probably occur somewhat frequently.)

We are looking to put ourselves and the department in the most defensible position while simultaneously supporting in every possible manner making the policies a living document, one that is ever present and which because it is known we increase the likelihood of its being followed.

Is it important enough to say that an officer who does not know the HR/CT policies should not be allowed out on the street? To me, knowledge of these policies must be comprehensive since every effort to reduce any potential problems with these twelve tasks must be reduced, and something more than mere "familiarity" is necessary. Officers should never have to admit they did not know a HR/CT policy, and thus performed a task incorrectly. No officer queried during a deposition should ever exhibit confusion about the policy requirements. Testing on the policies might accompany the review.

This exercise might seem as an injudicious use of time, but let's examine the benefits. If this step is taken, the department has irrefutable proof that it was not deliberately indifferent to the adequate training of its officers in light of the assigned tasks, the most solid of defenses for **Canton** and **Monell** suits. That step in combination with other factors (training records, quality supervision, and when necessary remediation) might impede or stop altogether any attack by the plaintiff's attorney on the department. Certainly we cannot deny that the repetition of, and emphasis on these policies, will have some positive effects on some of the officers.

4. Short videos on HR/CT policies

I believe that the chief, the policymaker, should make twelve short (3-5 minutes) videos on each one of the HR/CT policies. In these videos the chief would summarize the main points especially the policy statement and other prominent requirements. The department would designate each month of the year for one of these HR/CT policies, showing the videos at roll calls a number of times during that month. January might be for use of force, February for pursuits, etc.

One cannot miss the impact of a video featuring the chief of police speaking directly to the members of the department, emphasizing policy and the standards. Visually a strong performance is more striking that a lot of paper saying pretty much the same thing. For pursuits the video might have the chief say something such as the following:

> "February is dedicated to the topic of pursuits. I want to emphasize that when contemplating the initiation of a pursuit that each officer must balance the risk to himself and to others against the perceived need to apprehend the violator. When applying this balance, it is our policy not to initiate a pursuit for any non-continuing traffic violation or for any misdemeanor offense. Even when a pursuit is initiated for an appropriate reason every officer is reminded to continue balancing

the risk which might increase dramatically in certain areas like school zones against that need to apprehend.

"Our policy requires officers to communicate the reason for the pursuit at the time when it is started. Under no circumstances in our community will officers perform any PIT maneuvers except for the most serious of reasons. At the initiation of any pursuit audible and visible warning devices must be turned on, and if turned off officers must obey all traffic regulations as they no longer have emergency vehicle status according to state law."

I hope you get the idea, three to five minutes summarizing, not reading, the major points in the policy. At some future point in a lawsuit, these videos can be strong evidence to protect the department. Let's not overlook that it might also serve as a reminder about the policy's requirements for all of the officers.

There are obvious benefits to this approach:

1. the chief can be depicted vigorously reinforcing certain points in the policies.
2. in showing the videos a couple of times monthly the chief can again show how adequately the topics were emphasized. The roll call topic for the entire month of February was the policy on pursuits. And so on for the rest of the year's schedule.
3. suppose an officer in the opinion of a supervisor has come close to or actually violated the pursuit policy.Then to remind this officer about a particular facet of one of the HR/CT policies, a supervisor could require that he/she review the video on that subject. This can be recorded as "remedial training" or "corrective action" taken by that supervisor.

5. Command staff consensus training

Due to varying interpretations and applications of policies even at the command staff level there is not unanimity. In most cases it is after an event that command staff pore over the policies, if they do it at all. Usually when an incident occurs, it would be Internal Affairs or Professional Standards that researches every article in the policy and then applies it to the situation at hand.

I suggest that when a new policy is issued, or there is a revision in a HR/CT policy that the chief convene a staff meeting and given the subject of the policy, he/she would present a scenario, using a dashcam video from this department or one available from other sources or even written scenarios.

While it is constantly argued that "every situation is different" still there are similarities. The video or the scenario is meant to provoke discussion led by the policymaker. Having shown the video the chief would ask different members of the command staff if what the anonymous officer on the video did was within policy. Suppose it was a video of a pursuit. Directions from the chief might be:

1. apply our policy to this particular video.
2. was the pursuit initiated in keeping with our policy?
3. was the PIT maneuver appropriate at that point given the nearby cars?
4. was the force used to control the subject within our policy?

The policy represents the directives and guidelines from policymakers who have to make sure that as many as possible see its ramifications and applications. Therefore, as the various members of the command staff respond to these queries, the chief has a responsibility to guide them saying: "No, I don't see it that way. I don't agree with the officer's initiation of the pursuit for this reason." The chief variously could also say: "Yes, that is the perfect application of the policy" or "Check section V, d,3 and apply that to the video."

The goal of the meeting is to reach a little more uniformity in the application of the policy, that after five or ten videos culled from TV shows or other sources, the staff would leave the room with a better sense of the mind of the policymaker and would be able to speak more intelligently and uniformly about the requirements. This process forces the chief and command staff to articulate the application of the policy to incidents before they actually happen. Yes, it might also surface the opinions of individual staff members who are not in agreement with the policy; once the chief knows this it can be discussed at this meeting or left for a subsequent one-on-one session.

Ideally one of the staff members seated around the table will be assigned the task of using the same process with the lieutenants and sergeants and then the officers. Questions will be answered; it is a form of training in that policy, and greater uniformity in application and performance should be achieved.

Another benefit is: through this process any apparent contradictions or even mistakes in the policy might surface.

It is surprising how few people in a department actually are familiar with the policies. I have on a number of occasions worked with really sharp, highly educated personnel in research and planning, or professional standards. Ask them a question about certain policies and their response will be: "Well, let me check." If they don't know it, and they probably were the ones who actually put the words on paper for the chief, how do we expect all the other members of the department to know it?

6. HR/CT policies as part of all training

In many instances policies are seldom part of the official training curriculum for the BLET. They are only sporadically touched on in all the instances of in-service training. Take for example the training of officers for the use of tasers. In going over the materials provided by the vendors it is impossible for them to include a treatment of the use of force policies. Most of this taser training is provided to officers from a variety of departments with differing language and texts so that the instructors must avoid mentioning the policy requirements.

I recommend that any training whatsoever that touches on any aspects of the HR/CTs must include treatment of that policy and how it directly impacts the performance of that task. Once again if the training curriculum and lesson plans are discovered in litigation, the policymaker is seen as using every means possible to promulgate the policy.

7. HR/CT policies as part of reviews

To have the message of the HR/CT policies remain ever present as the standard of the department, these policies should be part of the review of every incident touching on these twelve critical topics. Encouragement should be given to have officers refer to pertinent parts of these policies in their incident reports. With a hoped for greater familiarity with the policies, incident reports could be strengthened with occasional exact quotations from the policies.

8. Training/testing for HR/CTs

I believe that computer-assisted training and testing if desired can be arranged for these policies with results posted to officers' training files.

9. Commentaries for discipline and commendation

Whenever discipline, remedial training, or commendations are issued, the relevant parts of the HR/CT policies should be referenced.

The common view of policy

While policies are seen as a necessity for the administration, this opinion is not universal down at the operational level. Some officers see it as a "C.Y.A." ploy by the administration and the command level personnel. (This might result because when administrators publish a policy, many then wipe their hands, and feel their job is mostly done since they have encapsulated all the standards in writing and they can go on to something else.) The message interpreted at the operational level is that policies mainly apply to them alone, because they are in the operational world; the policies attempt to regulate what they can do on the streets, and those policies might be seen as a prop for supervision that falls short of what is really should be.

This perception of policy at the operational level generates the view of policy as a "gotcha process" for the administration because officers think there is always something in the manual that can be thrown at them. Policy is never flexible where it could be and in some agencies is draconically enforced.

Policy as a protection for officers

Policy is the basis for qualified immunity which basically means that if an officer follows a proper policy, one that on its face has nothing unconstitutional in it or is not diametrically opposed to standards which any officer should know, then that officer can be granted qualified immunity during the course of a lawsuit. The officers were acting in good faith when they followed the policy. So if officers can hold up the policy in one hand and the incident report in the other hand and it is obvious that one follows the guidance in the other, qualified immunity should be their cover. Following the policy in effect is the officers' bulletproof vests offering protection from liability. Policy should be sold on the basis of that benefit.

Types of policies

Policies to me fall into four discernible categories which are:

1. formal
2. informal
3. operational
4. official

Let's look at each one and see how an evolution can take place; a different application of the policy evolves from its original context and meaning.

Formal

The formal policy is the written policy, issued by the policymaker. We can presume that it has all the characteristics of a solid policy, based on professional standards, complete and constitutional. It stands as the requirements for all officers to follow in performing those specific tasks and resides in the departmental policy manual.

Informal

Invariably in those days when policies were read out at roll calls by a supervisor, in the most subtle of ways there were certain spins placed on it by the manner and demeanor of the supervisor when explaining or commenting on it to the officers. This would happen even when copies of each new policy were placed in the officers' mail boxes, either the physical ones or their electronic version. Somehow the real meaning and direction of the policy were subverted by a wink, or a nod, or a facial expression or by comments that evinced the message: this is really not the way we do things. The policy had started its metamorphosis into something not intended by the author of the policy.

If you have ten sergeants distributing a policy at roll calls and then commenting on it, how many interpretations do you have? Once again the argument is made that at every level there must be attempts made to make the understanding of the policy uniform. If you have three shifts, how many police departments do you have? Or if you have six precincts, how many departments do you have?

Operational

Once out on the street the officers perform their assigned tasks in a particular manner. It could be exactly as the policy was written or it could be something different, something less than strict conformity to the written or formal policy, or conduct helped along by the informal messages conveyed by a supervisor in presenting the policy to the roll call. There is an erosion of the policy that occurs from the original meaning because "that is the way it is done out here on this shift."

Official

The courts look for the official policy of the department, and will hold the department responsible for it regardless of the proper and appropriate wording in the formal policy. If the court sees that there is racial profiling in traffic stops, or if it sees through a presentation replete with data on uses of force against minorities, there are easily discernible patterns that constitute constitutional violations, then the court will hold the agency responsible for what is actually being performed on the street. That will be the department's policy and it will be labeled the "official" policy, - just as much as if it were written up and placed in the policy manual.

Formal into official

If the formal policy does not become the official policy, little progress can be accomplished and the levels of protection from liability are minimized. The strategy of the policymaker and the various levels of supervision is to make the official policy so visible and so prominent that in the process it transcends even the unconscious efforts by lower level supervisors to thwart its correct interpretation and application even if accomplished unintentionally.

In each agency the question must be asked: "What do we have to do to make the formal policy the official policy?" If the formal policy is based on solid professional standards its implementation on the street will make it the official agency policy. This is no easy task, but not doing it only serves to weaken the department's protection, and make the whole corpus of the manual an empty document. Instead, make it a living document, one that is carried out on the streets.

Plaintiffs' attorneys are well aware of the possible faulty process existent in many departments. When an incident comes to their attention followed by their filing a lawsuit, it is to their advantage to pursue policy (formal and operational) to see if they can prove the official policy departs dramatically from the written or formal one. Decisions in the courts have been based on judicial proceedings stating that there was an official policy of employing excessive force against minorities because of the manner in which complaints were investigated with apparent blanket findings that excessive force was not used. It's the consistent pattern of what officers do on the street that could be found to be the official policy of the agency.

General Patton on policy

The man so notorious for wanting his orders carried out exactly and to the letter leaves us part of his philosophy when he says:

> "Issuing an order is 10%. The remaining 90% consists in proper and rigorous execution of the order."

Now Patton's "orders" are our "policies." The 90% for us falls into the functions of training, supervision and corrective action/discipline. General Patton wasn't one to trifle with people who dallied in carrying out his orders; he realized that to achieve the necessary objectives he had to be certain that the directives issued for the campaign be followed. Probably if you asked him, George would say that for him the remaining 90% was similar to ours for once he had said something there were no excuses for not obeying.

Most police managers and executives when surveyed agree with Patton about the 10%/ and 90% breakdown, but when asked what was the balance in practice in their departments, for most police chiefs, the answer came back closer to 90% and 10%. What are the implications to the profession if this is valid? I think the message is that too often when a policy is issued executives feel that everyone will fall in line. The mere existence of the policy will muster conformity to it, and the desired protections will fall into place. Not so, decidedly not so. What is undeniable: the hardest work and the greatest efforts come after the policy is issued!

It can only be seen that with the issuance of the policy there must be a continuum, a combination of managerial and supervisory responsibilities all focused on making sure the policy is followed exactly. Just as much as Patton would not leave off after the issuance of an order, we, too, cannot rest without devoting even more effort <u>after</u> the policy is disseminated. In fact many more times the effort to guarantee that it is followed.

CHAPTER 11

SIX-LAYERED LIABILITY PROTECTION SYSTEM

"The mark of a successful organization is not whether it has problems but whether it has the same problems it had last year."
                                                        -John Foster Dulles

From its publication in the **Police Chief** magazine in mid-1990, the article "The Six-Layered Liability Protection System," has been seen as a process for reining in lawsuits and raising performance levels. The process has been accepted in many quarters as a practical and effective approach to deal with the troublesome problem of pervasive liability. It gives us a plan, a template, and an overview of how to manage this troublesome problem.

The "Six Layers" process can address a particular task, for example the introduction and use of tasers, or a review of high speed pursuits, or finally a department-wide approach to encompass all tasks and services provided by a police agency. Be it a task, an audit, or a macrocosmic review the agency applying the Six Layers develops a picture showing the quality of performance and the areas which need attention.

As a template, use of the Six Layers can provide a form of strategic planning addressing the major critical areas while a systemic improvement of all of those layers with a commitment to improve each one individually serves as a format for strengthening them. Of course it is strongly recommended that reinforcement efforts on all six layers be accomplished simultaneously.

By analogy the Six Layers are akin to an officer's bulletproof vest. The Six Layers are a department's Liability Proof vest protecting it from lawsuits either by eliminating any threat or by minimizing it once an action has been filed. The efficacy of the Six Layers comes through the multiplicity of the layers, not in any one layer. (Too often nowadays, we feel secure when a measurable improvement in policies as a result of accreditation lulls us into a false sense of security. All layers must be improved simultaneously.) When all six are implemented as sturdily and completely as possible, the maximum protection is assured.

What follows will be a discussion of the Six Layers as they relate to policing. Even a cursory glance at them will establish the belief that the Six Layers could be used for multiple areas of local government.

1. The First Layer: Policy

In police organizations there is the obligation of providing administrative direction to all members. Someone is labeled as the policymaker, be it the chief of police alone, or the chief with the review and consent of the local city council. Of course there is the variant of having the council approve policies and then let the police executive determine procedures. What emanates from these sources is variously called policies, procedures, directives, standard operating procedures, or rules and regulations.

What is clear is that public organizations are required to have encapsulated in manuals the standards of care for their profession. Why? The reasons are to:

1. set the standards for performance of all of their activities
2. guide the members of the organization as to the reasons why a task is performed the way it is
3. lay out the method of performing the task, and
4. if necessary hold members responsible for not performing it correctly.

The correct, appropriate dissemination of these policies then allows the organization, in holding members accountable for their actions, to take disciplinary or corrective action.

Policies are based on the principle of foreseeability. Put simply this means that if the executive is going to require that the members perform certain tasks, then in the role of policymaker, he/she must provide direction as to how the task is to be performed.

So, the executive in foreseeing the tasks to be performed, must provide this direction prior to the expected performance of the tasks.

Too often policy is reactive; it is developed after an incident has occurred, and is seen as a means of preventing future mistakes in performing that task. Some organizations have been able to label a particular policy as the "Officer Jones" policy, for he made some mistake, handled a task incorrectly, caused a public reaction and in the wake of the reaction, a policy is needed. It is categorically unfair not to have the policies in place prior to the required performance of the task.

Not issuing policies in a timely manner allows certain customs and practices to become imbedded in the organization's operations only making it more arduous for the executive to change to a more professionally acceptable approach.

2. The Second Layer: Training

The criticality and the multiplicity of the tasks placed on the shoulders of our officers are daunting. A quick glance through the Basic Law Enforcement Training curriculum would bear out this conclusion. Look more closely at the block titled "Legal Training," where a vast expanse of law, statutes and even ordinances in some academies is laid out in a seventy hour block of time.

I would hold that most of this legal training, if learned at all suffices to get trainees through the unit's tests, but in few cases is it really known to the recruits. They don't know how to employ these laws correctly against those subjects who flaunt them. Furthermore I would hold that new officers learn the law from the steps taken and actions observed on the street by the example of their fellow officers. They become accustomed to the laws and the accompanying levels or categories by the hands-on-experience when they are sworn officers.

Training in the academies emphasizes knowledge of laws, procedures, and the necessary skills such as cuffing, takedowns, self-defense, and firearms training toward the eventual goal of qualification with the weapon. I say that high level performance comes more likely from the combination of knowledge, skills and decision making expressed in a formula such as:

High Level Performance = knowledge + skills + good decision making[2]

Debate exists about the efficacy of judgmental/discretionary shooting or shoot/don't shoot technology. Some say it is quite effective; other state it is only marginally so. But if it helps some officers prepare for the eventuality when they might have to use deadly force, I think it is worth it. But there is a lesson here. If the exercises are beneficial it is as a result of the improvement in decision making, i.e. when to use the knowledge and skill. To me it seems logical that training should have not only shoot/don't shoot sessions, but pursue/don't pursue, arrest/don't arrest, search/don't search, spray/don't spray, and stop/don't stop. If our trainees and officers have all the knowledge and skill they need (this point is debatable), then they need assistance to make the right decisions as to when to use that skill. Reflect on any number of lawsuits and you may discover that a remarkable number of them would not have occurred if officers made the right decisions. So this factor in training must be emphasized. Furthermore decisions made on a daily basis must be objectively reviewed and guidance must be given to guarantee that they are the right decisions. That emphasis will certainly affect the number of lawsuits.

A review of most basic law enforcement curricula would not show that the decision-making component, if included, is addressed adequately. Queries to officers usually state that knowledge and skills are emphasized with little if any time spent on decision making. Recruits have to be able to experience the application of their legal training in extensive scenarios where the mistakes are not nearly as costly as later on.

While lawsuits are generated frequently on high level uses of force or accidents, arrests, injuries and/or deaths resulting from the emergency operation of vehicles, there are many more minor actions of officers that mire a department in prolonged litigation.

It seems the more serious the offense, for example the robber running from the bank with a gun in his hand who raises it toward a responding officer, does not require prolonged decision making. However, the lower level offenses, like disorderly conduct require a more complex calculus of considerations, greater exhibition of decision making, and an ability to articulate the reasoning for using force in reports and eventually in court. In one sense the more serious the offense, the less discretion that has to be exercised in the officer's response; the less serious the offense, the more discretion is involved and the more the officer must think through the decision as to the proper action. The officer must act more deliberately in these situations.

Of course, there is no denying the criticality of some serious offenses: encountering the armed robber or the felony traffic stop. My point is that it may be difficult to evaluate the exact parameters of disturbing the peace and defending that judgment while explaining the reasons for the action. A simple disorderly conduct with loud and boisterous noise at night disturbing people present or in the area cost one city $90,000 plus $3,100,000 in legal fees when the inadequacy of the training and administrative components were factored in. Still officers had been making faulty decisions on these high frequency and low criticality incidents for some time dependent on the supervisors not spotting legal deficiencies in thousands of arrests over years.

Training must include intensive focus on the policies (we would call them the High Risk/Critical Task policies) that generate the greatest chances of liability. For the most part, Basic Law Enforcement Training (BLET) does not include training on any policies except for some inclusion of force and pursuits. Why? Law enforcement agencies do not have uniform policies; therefore BLET sessions having trainees from a broad reach of agencies, cannot train to the policies.

When a new officer joins a department, and there is a Field Training Officer (FTO) program, there is allegedly a daily check on "knowledge of policies" usually understood as those policies implicated in the incidents experienced on that particular shift. (What happens if the day's calls-for-service run the gamut from boisterous parties, to someone running a stop sign, to a false burglar alarm. There is minimal systemic coverage of the most important policies nor of all of the policies.)

If it didn't happen on the shift, then the relevant policy knowledge is not observed by the FTO. Even in the best of FTO programs there are serious gaps in the attempts to assess the new officer's knowledge of policies. If this evaluation by the FTO were adequate, another flaw in this approach exists. The evaluation is uneven; certain sections of the relevant policies might be highlighted and other sections, also important are overlooked.

Policies are not the subject of training, nor is there any certitude that at any point from the first emergence of the new officer to veteran status that the most important policies are known. Where do we teach policies? We can track on whether or not an officer received the policies, but can we say they know the policies?

While it has not yet been the subject of much scrutiny when it comes to litigation, I expect that in time not only will the contents of the training be more closely examined, but a neglected area will become of more interest to plaintiffs. That area is the quality of testing in the BLET which does not exhibit content and testing validity. What passes for testing in some training environments is rudimentary, and little can be said about how much of the training is actually retained. Most testing is multiple choice, fill-in-the-blank, matching columns.

Yes, scenario-based training forces trainees to use their knowledge and skills, and to do some thinking. Can it be increased? Yes, probably in most areas. Regrettably the opponents of lengthening the academy to allow for an enhancement or expansion of the curriculum are in some cases the department executives who want their new officers on the street as soon as possible. Or there are the severe restrictions on funding sources to provide more staff, or to have them teach longer blocks of topics.

Someone has said: "Police training is a process where the notes of the instructor become the notes of the instructor without passing through the minds of either." There is a lot of teaching for the test, and a hesitancy to flunk a recruit. Are the generally high grades in the BLET the result of good training, a grasp of the concepts, or rather simple test questions? I have yet to see any questions where the response requires the trainee or officer to write out a logically developed essay answer.

Having touched on testing in the BLET, I would raise the topic for all in-service and specialized training. I met a supervisor from a department who said: "We have a SPLAT team; that is Special Personnel Lacking Any Training." Quite an admission in a jocular manner and in furthering the conversation as he catalogued the deficiencies in training, there was a diminishing humorous character to his comment There is seldom any testing presented in all of these courses. Training in most cases is an exposure to the subject with little evaluation of the retention or grasp of what has been presented.

3. The Third Layer: Supervision

As mentioned before, supervision means to "look over" or to observe with the obvious requirement to correct if what is being observed is not performed properly. We have already mentioned something about the problems of supervisors standing with a foot in two worlds, that of the officer at the operational level and that of an extension of management. We have heard how they are uniquely unprepared for this demanding role. Finally it is almost universal that few supervisors are actually trained for this role before they are thrust, it might be said *in medias res,* or right into the middle of things.

Supervision must be supportive of the officers, and supportive of good and high level performance. The essence of the role is to assist officers in becoming the very best that they can be, and to counsel them when necessary when they are falling short of standards.

4. The Fourth Layer: Corrective Action, Remediation, Discipline, and Commendations

Gallagher's Principle #8 states that "Discipline in its reactive mode is in essence a failure on the part of the proactive (policy and training) and active (supervision) components of the Six Layers."

Maybe that principle is an overstatement for it presumes a level of perfection in the proactive and active processes that affect performance. Discipline and corrective action just as much as supervision will always be present. But it all returns to the question as to how we improve performance. One state attorney general even mentioned in his directive to all the state's law enforcement agencies that in lieu of outright discipline we should try counseling, retraining, enhanced supervision, oral reprimands, and performance notices. Nothing wrong with that at all. Those are the necessary methods available to us.

Performance is improved proactively before we allow the new officer on the street by means of policy and basic training. Once out on the street, on a day-to-day basis we rely on quality supervision to improve performance. Reactively performance is influenced by inspections, audits, evaluations, counseling, commendations and recognition, remediation and yes, discipline all coming after the fact.

In our current management of police organizations, the role of inspections and audits as a regular part of doing our business has assumed an almost non-existent role. When prodded by an event, an incident which causes us to be concerned, or by a lawsuit, we may indulge in some inspectional functions mainly on demand for production of documents. In receiving the report, do we act on its recommendations? (Would we want inspections on new cars only after serious defects were discovered?)

I hold that if there were more inspections, more counseling on the quality of performance, more recognition and commendations there might be less need for corrective action. Inspections will indicate how well our officers are performing and allow executives to make decisions that will elevate performance even more. Why? We can emphasize through the findings, through the discussions and through reviews how well our officers are performing. By doing this we are showing what our expectations are for performance meeting standards, for correct adherence to policies, and for recognizing the individual officer. Too often the attention goes to the reprimand or the discipline, highlighting performance short of the standard. By recognition and commendation we recognize what is on or above the standard, and thus we teach what we want officers to do.

What occurs too often is an example of the NBA maxim of "no harm, no foul." If there is no negative outcome, then the action passes without comment. However if that is the operative principle, and no action is taken to correct some shortcoming, statistically every repetition of that act brings us closer to the time when it will have a negative outcome. By not taking action, a subtle message goes out that the practice is acceptable.

Again I feel that it comes down to the supervisory style present. I believe that supervisors should actively seek out the good performances of subordinates, and comment on it such as:

> "Officer Jones, I just read over that report you did on the incident over at 3424 Fourth St. last night. I must say you handled a difficult situation superbly well. Keep up the good work."

The supervisor who makes this informal recognition a part of his or her *modus operandi* will establish a different and more positive relationship than the person who only communicates with subordinates when they have done something wrong.

Performance short of standards or those surpassing standards for the most part must be documented, not necessarily in the officer's personal file, but possibly in a supervisor's notebook to aid in evaluations and in the case of litigation to prove that the supervisor took action, i.e. counseled, reprimanded, or recommended discipline. Supervisors must review the dashcams regularly, because there is no better manner of seeing an officer in action. Yet how often is this done?

The Fifth Layer: Constant Review and Revision

The key to this layer is that anything relating to performance must be reviewed and any needed revision made. The ongoing review would include data, studies, and incident reports to glean any morsel of information that can improve performance, help implement changes, better the quality of services, indicate topics or tasks which need additional training, or discover any disturbing trends for individual officers, an entire shift, or the full department. This review can also document the solid and high quality professional activity of officers and special units.

Currently one of the most commonplace forms of review of police performance is that of the internal affairs or professional standards process to deal with complaints, for the most part filed by citizens. The process as commonly found around the country is uneven, incomplete, and not totally professional. One of the most comprehensive guides or *vademecums* which is now going into its fourth edition is the **Law Enforcement Administrative Investigations: A Manual Guide** by Lou Reiter, (ret.) deputy chief, LAPD. Another recommended volume is **Internal Affairs Investigations: A Guide for the Investigator** by Frank Rodgers, (ret.) lieutenant colonel, NJSP. Both texts contain models of all the essential forms for the complete investigation.

As mentioned previously the police profession generally is not attuned to critically examining data. It reposes in our computers in raw form with little done to piece it out and separate the chaff from the wheat.

The ongoing review can forestall certain forays by plaintiffs' attorneys to use data against the department while offering it as a solid defense in certain instances. Finally it provides valuable information for management to base changes on a solid evaluation of the data.

The review is only one-half of what is necessary for it must lead to a revision of practices, an increase or change in training, the elimination or formation of a special unit, the identification of potential troublesome officers or activities.

Many agencies when an incident occurs and there is a subsequent lawsuit, hesitate to examine their practices and make changes at that time, fearing, needlessly, that it could affect the current case. Well, Jack Ryan, J.D., of the highly regarded Legal and Liability Risk Management Institute elucidated this point by saying:

> "that is covered in the rules of evidence and these changes are referred to as 'self-critical analysis' or 'subsequent remedial measures.' The public policy behind these rules of evidence is that it would not be in anyone's best interest to wait to fix the problem until the lawsuit ends since doing so may lead to more injuries by the very mechanism that needs to be fixed. The rules contemplate fixing it right away so that the injuries are cut off. The incentive is no future suits and the subsequent remedial measure cannot be used against the party being sued."

Ryan went on to say that in a major case involving the friendly fire shooting of a Providence, R.I. officer, Cornel Young, that he (Ryan) in his role as training director of the Providence Police Department rewrote the policy on off-duty action which was significantly different from the "always armed, always on duty" policy. In two trials the judge did not allow the admission of the new policy ruling it was a "subsequent remedial measure."

The lesson here for all of us is when an incident occurs decide what the professional standards would require, make the changes and get the officers trained in the changes.

After an incident, some departments say in alleged excessive force complaints against a person, delay taking any action, delay completing the Internal Affairs case until the end of the civil process. But what happens if before the termination of the first civil suit, there is another similar incident of alleged excessive force and the executive again delays? And possibly a third instance?

Far-fetched? Maybe, but the point is that in delaying, or doing nothing we have a clear case of administrative inaction and no message going out to the officers that conduct similar to that involved in this case will be rigorously investigated and disciplinary action will be taken. This inaction in the face of a pattern of alleged constitutional violations strengthens the plaintiff's case and erodes the department's defensive position.

Organizationally we become so afraid of the consequences of doing the right thing in a timely manner that we delay and allow a "pattern or practice" of overlooking this violation which could exacerbate this string of incidents into a **Monell** claim of a practice of constitutional violations. In the end the department and its executive are in a much worse situation.

The Sixth Layer: Legal Support, Counsel and Training

As has been mentioned previously, the block of legal training in the Basic Law Enforcement Training (BLET) compresses a tremendous amount of convoluted legal principles and the elements of close to a hundred criminal offenses of felonies and misdemeanors into seventy hours with little time to allow officers to feel comfortable with their knowledge of the "law" and how to apply it.

Building on the inadequate base of the BLET, officers are constantly bombarded with newly passed local ordinances, recently enacted state statutes, and of course new case law coming down from the state and federal levels.

"Law" enforcement officers must know the law. Is our system at the basic level and down the line for in-service and legal training updates sufficient to handle this burden? I think not. Legal updates are usually reserved, when they are available, for an annual training session that might include other mandatory topics not directly related to the law, e.g. child abuse, domestic violence or other issues imposed by the state legislatures or the state police training commission.

Legal updates are usually presented by a member of the district attorney's staff, an attorney who assists police department on defense in civil cases, and in some cases an academy staff member, not an attorney, who handles the block of legal training. Certainly these people are qualified but it is the process of getting across the message that is flawed. Conceivably legal update training might be scheduled ten to twelve months after a law is passed, or on the civil side after a case has been decided.

But look at the other side. Plaintiffs' attorneys are motivated to keep up with new decisions and their profession itself has in place considerable resources to inform them of developments. They can act almost immediately on new directions offered to them in case law.

Furthermore, for us legal update training by attorneys in some cases is not oriented enough to a non-attorney class, emphasizing frequently the legal niceties in the decision which are not relevant to the audience. Police officers are action- or task-oriented, performing one task after another many of which have legal underpinnings. Legal update training must take this into consideration.

Minimally, legal update training for police must emphasize four points:

1. How does the new law, the new decision in this case affect how the officers perform their tasks?
2. Does the new law or case decision make it more difficult or easier for the officers to perform their tasks?

3. In what specific areas does the new law or case decision require them to change the manner in which they were performing their assigned tasks?
4. What policy, procedural or training changes have to be made?

Of course we would not want restrictions to be placed on the breadth and reach of the presentation but minimally the training must focus on the officer-in-the-street environment. It must be made practical in the field operations arena.

In some states, the attorney general will issue a lengthy memo addressing the issues in a new law or case decision. This memo is sent to all the county prosecutors who append a few more pages of commentary. Finally this package is sent to the law enforcement executives in that county, and distributed to the officers or posted on line or still in some cases on a bulletin board. While the contents are excellent and very much on point, it is quite indigestible for the expected audience.

I feel that associations of state police executives, state police officer standards and training (POST) commissions must provide competent legal update training in a timely manner. For the majority of our police departments with their limited number of officers there must be a better process for providing legal updates, since these smaller departments cannot provide it themselves.

Assessing Your Department

I have very frequently employed an exercise based on the Six Layered Liability Protection System (SLLIPS) in training classes for supervisors, managers, and chiefs. The results can illustrate some target areas and while the results are not definitive they can highlight what must be addressed.

Directions

With the Six Layers listed below, on a scale of 1 (lowest) and 10 (highest) give a score to your department and then list one specific step which you could take to make it better insulated against liability, to raise the score from say seven to eight, or eight to nine.

Six Layers	Score 1-10	Action Step to Increase Protection
Policy	_____	Action step_____
Training	_____	Action step_____
Supervision	_____	Action step_____
Discipline/ Remediation	_____	Action step_____
Review and Revision	_____	Action step_____
Legal Training	_____	Action step_____

Usually Policy and Training score a seven or eight, Supervision six to eight depending on the audience, Discipline a six, Review and Revision a five and Legal Training always the lowest, in some cases a 0-3. On a couple of occasions I have been asked if the responding supervisors could give Legal Training a negative score!

Another Exercise

I have also utilized the following challenge to course participants but mainly though for police executives. Think of a particularly horrendous incident that might occur in your jurisdiction, such as a mass shooting, an attack on a school, an off-duty and possibly intoxicated officer involved in an argument resulting in shooting, a high speed pursuit with crash and fatalities, the kidnapping of a young girl. Get the idea?

Realize that this is going to cause you a tremendous amount of stress and push your resources to the limit. For any one of these events what are the steps that you would have wanted to put in place prior to that incident so that under the circumstances you can get a good night's sleep that following night, that serious exposure to any possible liability is thwarted by the defenses you have put in place.

Whatever those steps are, implement them as soon as possible in anticipation of some event similar to the above list. Don't let the regret of not doing enough sour your day.

Success

Success comes from practice and repetition. The profession without a doubt cannot truly improve in its confrontation with liability by going at it piecemeal, i.e. a small improvement in policies, a couple of hours of additional training, sending a supervisor to a training session, or reviewing dashcam videos after questionable incidents. Success comes if the process of the Six Layers (SLLIPS) is implemented with the objective of raising each layer to the highest point possible. While addressing energies to all Six Layers, we must realize that the push for excellence allows for no respites. It is demanding, it is constant, and if totally implemented it is the <u>process</u> that will diminish the burden of liability. It is the absence of any other true process that has us so perplexed; so much in a quandary in searching for a way through the thickets of liability. Commit to SLLIPS. The alternative to it requires that we shoulder this ever increasing burden for all of our careers.

CHAPTER 12

CASE STUDY: APPLYING THE SIX LAYERS (SLLIPS)

"In a value-neutered society, could police become the exemplars of values?"

-Chief Neil Behan, (ret.)

In this chapter, an actual police incident is summarized. To show the application of the **Six Layered Liability Protection System** it is suggested that after reading the summary, you go through the **Six Layers** and apply them to this incident and to the continuum of steps to see how well your department is prepared for, and is defensible against any possible lawsuit.

(I would say that where there is the possibility of litigation, even before any actual filing, that you utilize the **Six Layers** to evaluate your stance vis a vis possible litigation.)

As chief of police or manager of your department, apply the Six Layers of Liability Protection, listing the steps you would take prior to the introduction of the taser and for the first two years that officers employed it.

The Incident

This incident occurred just before midnight on October 30, 2010 when dispatch notified Officer Mason of a domestic violence situation in progress at 256 Blue Road. Officers Mason and Wilson both answered the call in separate cars. The department had only 18 officers; Wilson was just about to go off duty, Mason was just coming on.

This address was not unknown to the department's officers because since 1999 there were a total of 41 complaints emanating from this address and/or the Colgan family. Mrs. Anita Colgan made seventeen of them and Mr. Daniel Colgan called in thirteen times. Even Avery, their son, was no stranger to calling the department for starting at ten years old he made seven calls to include the one on October 30, 2010. For example prior to this night, the parents had called in to report a dead deer in their back yard.

However, in examining the seven calls that Avery made it is obvious that he was very protective of his mother (and later his younger brother) when their father was violent toward them. This culminated in his reporting the kicking of his younger brother on the night of October 30, 2010 when as he said: "Mom flipped out." On four of the occasions he notified the sheriff's department that his father had left the residence and had taken off in his truck. These facts were unknown to the responding officers.

The following details were all captured on the officers' dashcams. As Officer Mason slowed to identify the correct address, dispatch updated him that the subject was fleeing the scene in a truck. (Presumably Avery had alerted dispatch through another call.)

Daniel Colgan had a medical history of two heart attacks, one each in the previous two years, as well as a history of cocaine use. On this evening his BAC was 0.17 and he had some marijuana in his system. (These conditions were not known to the officers at the time of this incident.) Officer Mason's attempt to stop the vehicle was unsuccessful, as the driver of this truck, coming from 256 Blue Road disregarded the officer's blue lights. The officers turned around and initiated a pursuit with lights and siren. Having caught up with the fleeing truck the subject, now traveling at 60 mph. continued on, turning left on one road and then came to a stop in a gravel parking lot approximately 1.9 miles down the road.

Immediately, before the officers could even turn off their sirens, the driver exited the truck, moving back toward the officers' cars, yelling something unintelligible. What was understood was Colgan's calling out: "Go ahead and shoot me."

Neither lights and siren, nor the officers' lawful commands had gotten the subject to submit to the officers. Officer Mason felt concerned enough and somewhat threatened to the extent that he had his weapon drawn holding the man "at gun point."

Officer Wilson had aligned himself to Mason's left and had his taser drawn. To the officer, it was obvious that the man understood the verbal commands but he only shouted: "Go ahead and shoot me." The shouted commands were repeated; Colgan continued to wave his arms around outside of his jacket which was unzipped. Finally as Colgan moved closer to them, Mason directed Wilson to tase the man.

Wilson did as directed, hitting the subject with a five second deployment in the upper chest; Mr. Colgan then fell backwards. The officers closed immediately on the subject, who struggled somewhat while again mouthing unintelligible sounds attributed to the alcohol. In addition to the sounds the subject was making, he was moving his legs and body as the officers successfully cuffed him.

The officers started searching the man and Mason returned to his car to turn off the siren, prior to his intention of reading the man his Miranda warnings. He found the subject not moving and having irregular breathing, initially presumed to be the results of the alcoholic consumption.

The officers raised him to a sitting position, but the subject was limp and breathing was labored. No pulse could be located. An ambulance was requested; the officers removed the restraints and immediately hooked him up to the Automatic External Defibrillator, initiating CPR. The ambulance transported the subject to the hospital where he lingered for four months before dying.

Questions:

1. Policies:
- When were the policies on the use of the taser last updated?
- Did the policies include all the latest updates from Taser, Inc.?
- Did the use of force policy correctly position the taser on the Force Continuum?

- Did the totality of the circumstances present a valid threat to the officers?
- Did the officers actually feel threatened?
- Were all the policies relating to a use of force followed?
- Were all the required reports filed?

2. Training:
- Were these deputies and all other deputies certified in the use of the taser?
- Were all the memos from Taser, Inc. made a part of the training?
- Were all the deputies, even those certified some time ago, updated on more recent memos from Taser, Inc.?
- Was all of the training properly documented in each deputy's file?
- Were the deputies who conducted the training properly trained?
- Was their training updated as required?
- Were there any deputies carrying a taser without being trained?
- Were the deputies involved properly trained in the AED and CPR?
- Was the training adequate in use of force scenarios relating to the taser?

3. Supervision:
- Were supervisors immediately called to the scene?
- Did they take adequate charge of the scene?
- Did they notify the chain of command?
- Had supervisors found any uses of force involving tasers questionable?
- What was the follow-up on these identified problems?

4. Discipline, Reprimands, and Commendations:
- Had either of the deputies involved in this incident been disciplined for inappropriate uses of force? What level of force? How many times?
- If yes, was there any remediation assigned? What was it?
- Was it carried out? Was it documented?
- If no discipline were there any commendations for superior performance in high risk and critical tasks?

5. Review and Revision:
- Were all of the reports reviewed by supervisors?

- Were the required reviews of the incident conducted?
- Did the departmental use of force Review Board come out with findings?
- Were those findings in support of the deputies' use of force?
- Were the deputies' files reviewed to see if there were previous incidents of this nature? What were the findings of the reviews?
- What, if any, were the interactions which these deputies had with the subject previously?
- Are there any changes which should be made in the department's training for the use of the taser? For uses of force? For reviews of uses of force?
- Are there any changes which should be made in the policies on the use of the taser? On the use of force?
- Has the department collected data on the use of the taser since it was entrusted to our deputies?
- Has the data been analyzed?
- Does the data show any possible improper use of the taser?

6. Legal Training:
- Has the department updated the deputies on the case law on the use of the taser?
- Has there been updating on the case law on the use of force?
- Was the training conducted in a timely manner?

Conclusion

These six topics can be applied to any type of incident at any time. The framework of the **Six Layers** affords us a ready-made review and evaluation process. Moreover when there is an innovation in the department, the various **Six Layers** could be assigned to various supervisors and managers to have them staff one particular layer. One officer might be assigned to a review of policies, possibly requesting policies from other agencies.

Suggestion: a consortium of sorts could be developed, possibly composed of accredited agencies in different areas of the country, so that policies as they are revised could be shared almost automatically with all those in the group. Furthermore, with state accreditation associations there are ready sources of solid policy available.

CHAPTER 13

STEPS TO TAKE BEFORE AND AFTER LITIGATION

"Management is doing things right. Leadership is doing the right things."

-Peter Drucker and Warren Bennis

"You can avoid reality. But you cannot avoid the consequences of reality."

-Ayn Rand

Pre-litigation

The provision of law enforcement services involves the constant confrontation with a gamut of risks. There is little in policing that is not fraught with some risk. Police officers are expected to drive on occasion at high speeds, to use a variety of weapons that can seriously injure or kill a person, or to physically struggle to control a person. They are tasked with determining the appropriate times when they should restrict a person's freedom. To investigate properly they need to conduct searches. These actions generate responses. If in the opinion of the subject involved, these actions allegedly violated established norms, then there is a complaint and possibly a lawsuit.

Lawsuits in today's society's litigious climate can be expected. How do you prepare for the inevitable?

We would never want the consciousness about potential lawsuits to have officers hesitate to take appropriate action, to delay and hold back when they know they should be getting involved, or to not defend themselves when attacked. But this consciousness has to be on the minds of many officers; they know fellow officers who have gone through the stress of having their actions, taken under the need for split second decision-making in a particular incident, analyzed meticulously at the leisure of plaintiff's attorneys. There is always the element of second guessing, the thoughts that they "coulda, woulda, shoulda" done things differently.

While the reminders of lawsuits might be common, the fact remains that only a small percentage of officers is ever sued. Research shows that only one percent of those who file complaints actually sue. Still we owe it to our officers to prepare them for that eventuality, - if it ever comes. What steps can we take to put our officers in a better position to anticipate a lawsuit?

Not to make light of experiences that officers find so stressful, but by analogy they must realize that it could be said they litigate their cases in criminal court which is their home court as it were. Lawsuits take place in civil court where they are the away team; there are different rules and they are in different roles, for they are now defendants. The officers stand accused of some civil wrong and the very nature of the process in civil court places them in a defensive position.

I think it's quite simple: explain that following the departmental policies is critical to remaining free from litigation. Officers should train themselves not only in the physical skills but also in the constant awareness of actions that might go over the line. Constantly improve quality training centered particularly on those tasks which are more difficult and could lead more easily to the filing of lawsuits.

Officers and supervisors can learn from those around them - those in their department or in other departments, studying how they might have become involved in a lawsuit. Become a student of the liability process to learn what <u>must</u> be done and <u>how</u> it should be done.

One established and valid method of improving performance is to have after-action critiques, but critiques to "learn, not to blame." Officers can learn a tremendous amount from reviewing critical actions. The question might be asked: "Was the manner in which we handled that incident the best approach? Could we have handled it any better? What could be done to improve our performance?" These critiques are invaluable as training, for with these critiques officers have a ready file that they might be able to recall when they are faced with a similar situation. However, the profession first has to move away from associating critiques exclusively from the traditional search for someone to blame. Conduct them frequently and the process can uncover numerous officers who performed superbly under difficult conditions.

As mentioned previously our **Supervisor's Field Manual Checklist** was an attempt to get the best minds and the most experienced practitioners to list every single task that should be done during a number of challenging incidents. Review the incident with the use of the checklist with the objective of improving performance, not of singling out any one individual.

Going a step beyond after-action critiques the inspectional function long suffering from desuetude should be revived always with the goal of improving performance, of doing everything better. The best method of avoiding lawsuits is constantly seeking the highest level of performance of even the simplest tasks.

Take those steps.

Post-Litigation: Getting Your Money's Worth

A lot of money goes out when there is a lawsuit against a department: legal fees, officers' time to respond to requests for documents, personnel being deposed and absent from their regular assignments, and finally if it goes that far, the time spent sitting through the trial. Those are the costs if the department wins the case! Regardless of these costs, if the verdict goes against the department there is the additional financial burden of the judgment and the associated legal fees. That figure could be astronomical.

Seldom, if ever, do we get real value out of the expenditure of a considerable amount of money because when the case is decided, the officers' time is part of the departmental budget, and insurance coverage provides for the actual monetary outlay. Like a rock thrown into the water, there is an initial disturbance, ripples and then the smoothness of the water takes over.

Turning the lawsuit into a learning experience

In the aftermath of the suit this is a perfect time to use the focus of the suit, such as use of force, emergency operations of police vehicles, arrest procedures or searches to apply the **Six Layered Liability Protection System (SLLIPS)** to that topic.

Policies

Review the policies associated with this suit, especially the ones turned over to the plaintiff's attorney through discovery. Did the plaintiff's attorney highlight any part or component of the policies that should be deleted or changed? Did the policies referenced in the plaintiff's expert's report - and provided as attachments - offer the language that might improve our policy? Did the depositions of officers indicate that they were not conversant with the policies? When queried were they able to say they were trained in the policies? Could the officers explain how the policies provided guidance as to how they were to perform certain tasks? Did they follow the policies?

Training

Could we adequately prove that the officers were trained in the tasks related to this suit? Were there any aspects of training brought out by the plaintiff's attorney that we should consider changing? Or implementing? If we had to submit lesson plans could we find them? Were those lesson plans appropriate to support our case? Were we satisfied with our documentation of the training? If any tests were given could we justify the composition of the test questions?

Supervision

If supervisors were directly involved at the scene were their actions correct? Did the supervisor take charge, and make the correct decisions? Or give the correct orders? Was there anything that he/she could have done to improve the oversight of the incident? Does the supervisor's performance warrant special training for this supervisor? Or for all supervisors? Did the supervisor correctly review the incident reports? Did the supervisor require any corrections in the reports? Were those corrections essential? Would those corrections have improved our case?

Discipline, remediation or commendation

Was there any need for some form of discipline? Or for remediation? What action would have been appropriate? If any action was taken: discipline, remediation or counseling, was it documented? Did we check to find out if the officers involved had been involved in similar situations previously? Were the circumstances in this case repeated at some point in the past by other officers? If there is any type of repetition of circumstances is there a necessity to change/upgrade any policies? Or any training? Are there officers who performed perfectly in line with our policies? Or with our training? As exemplars of what we expect have we recognized them?

Review and revision

Have we reviewed the incident in its entirety? Have we critiqued the incident, critiqued to learn not to blame? Have we determined that there might have been a better way to handle the situation? Have we gotten every bit of value out of the incident and its aftermath? Is there a need to prepare our officers better for depositions? Or for court testimony in a civil trial? What has to be revised? Policies? Training? Style of supervision? Discipline? Remediation? If appropriate have we gathered some statistics surrounding this incident? Are there any trends developing? Have we kept data on similar type incidents? Have we analyzed the data? Have we used it to improve any part of our policies or training?

Legal advice and counsel

Were we satisfied with our legal defense? Did our attorney adequately prepare the officers for depositions? Or for trial? Did he/she keep the department informed of developments? Did our defense counsel provide us with an after-action-report? Did he/she bring up any other suggestions? Did the trial indicate any form of legal training necessary for our officers? To the extent discernible did our officers know the law relating to this case?

We are all so interested in not being sued, and even more so in not being sued successfully. But given the vagaries of the circumstances surrounding the incident and the inexplicable directions which a court or a jury might take, a loss might be suffered. It makes sense to get the most out of this loss, and learn from every aspect of it. It does not make sense to refuse to accept the verdict if that stance freezes us organizationally and administratively. I don't say embrace the verdict. What has taken place barring a successful appeal is going to stand. Milk that experience for anything that can make your department better prepared not to give the chance to another plaintiff to launch a suit, and certainly if launched not to lose another suit in court.

If the police were to receive a favorable verdict in every case, that would be a satisfactory goal. But we still have paid a lot to achieve it. However, wouldn't it be easier to win, not in court, but on the street? If any hope for the plaintiffs' attorneys to pick up cases was dashed by the initial performance of the officers, that would eliminate the unpleasantness and stress of all that would follow. Performance short of the best level according to standards only encourages the filing of a suit, for plaintiffs' attorneys prefer to have, like their TV, liability on demand.

Win in the street if at all possible. Don't feed the plaintiffs' attorney, starve them.

CHAPTER 14

OUR ALLIES: THE INSURANCE AND RISK MANAGEMENT POOLS

"The principle of organizational and personal change is gentle pressure, relentlessly applied."

-Lou Reiter, Asst. Chief, (ret) LAPD

"If we don't mind paying the price of doing business the way we are, then change nothing. If however, we don't want to pay that price, then we have to change the way we do business."

-Gallagher's Principles #9

Stop and think: the insurance and risk management pools have the same goals and objectives as do police departments: the avoidance of lawsuits and the diminution of any settlements or judgments in economic terms. The managers of the pools and their boards of directors are committed to reducing risks wherever possible. To accomplish this objective, they must forge a close working relationship with their member police departments. The available data are sparse but providing insurance coverage and some other services for their police agencies with the necessary defense costs and occasional settlements and judgments have to constitute the greatest outlay of their resources.

As such, it follows that we must be pragmatic to achieve what law enforcement wants, the decrease in the burden of liability and what the pools seek, the reduction in losses and a decrease in expenses to refund more to their members annually or to reduce the actual costs for the coverage.

There is no question about it; the pools have become one of the strongest supporters of law enforcement. But can this symbiotic relationship, as good as it is currently, be enhanced? Is there more that could be done in this cooperative arrangement? Can the pools become more active in assisting police, in identifying and addressing specific problems inherent in each pool? In specific departments? Particularly for smaller departments which constitute an overwhelming percentage of the pools' memberships, what services would make the struggle against liability more productive? If we were to survey a greater majority of the pools what are the additional services that they have implemented in the last three to five years that have directly assisted police to improve their defenses?

In providing or arranging for insurance coverage it is with the thought that the combined efforts of every pool member will be focused on the optimum strategies to further those goals. If police agencies don't like to be sued and even more to lose lawsuits, then they are of a like mind with the pools' management. But to truly diminish the number and frequency of lawsuits and subsequent losses there must be forged a solid determination and commitment to do whatever it takes, including some steps seemingly quite foreign to the present approaches. Certain methods and processes which have only provided a modicum of returns, but returns nevertheless, can be improved, or replaced by a new approach.

Those returns and savings have been readily accepted by pools and their members. And yes, the involvement of the pools has benefited law enforcement appreciably. My point: if totally committed to a reduction in losses, there are a number of additional steps which the pools must take, otherwise they will never realize their potential. If policing wants to do more to shake off the burden of liability, then it must agree to allow the introduction of more stringent risk management approaches with assistance from the pools.

I feel that much more can be accomplished in the processes for reducing liability, for getting it off the individual and collective backs of our police agencies. The question is: Are police agencies individually and collectively in their pools open and ready to take what might be seen as drastic steps which will help the profession reach the elusive tipping point where it is not the ordinary course of action for an agency to be sued successfully but rather the exception?

G. Patrick Gallagher

In querying police chiefs and their managers, they universally will admit that our efforts so far have not really been successful. Secondly they will say that the problem in their opinion is getting worse. Liability is a problem that is not decreasing but is growing in size. They declare that plaintiffs' attorneys are progressively getting more aggressive, and these chiefs will admit in more candid moments the whole problem is draining their energies and their attention.

The problem is systemic: the police profession does not have in place a total process for addressing this problem. The process, a series of actions toward a specific end, such as it is, is flawed in that it is incomplete. I have said it is like building a bridge across a river. Regardless of the quality of construction of supports and its underpinnings, the bridge does not achieve the objective of reaching the other side until it is completed. The foundations must be completed, the roadway smoothed, and then a greatly increased amount of success will be ours. The police profession should drive the liability process, not be driven by it.

Our opponents in the civil arena have a process in place, and we all will probably attest to their success in the last couple of decades. These plaintiffs' attorneys keep up with the evolution of case law pertaining to negligence and constitutional violations by police. They search around for the raw material essential to them: alleged police performance falling markedly below professional standards, they file a complaint and eventually a lawsuit, and move through the requisite steps in pursuing the case to a settlement or a judgment. They have learned in their local and regional environment the pressure and effort necessary to achieve a hoped for objective in many cases from liability-weary agencies and pools. With their coffers filled, they can then scan the environment for another target of opportunity. That is the manner in which their process works.

We can't deny that they work hard; they know the principles of their profession and the various stratagems that are most likely to make them successful. They have honed their abilities through countless depositions and endless days in court. Many are ambitious enough to study the literature and books describing the approaches used by the most successful attorneys; they attend conferences to develop new methods and means of winning in all their efforts. Has the police profession improved its ability to thwart their efforts? Has the profession studied and analyzed the data, determining the patterns of lawsuits and the causes that initiated them? Has that profession in the last two decades devised innovative methods of reducing the plaintiffs' attorneys' chances for success?

Yes, the police profession has taken some quantum steps spurred on by the national and state accreditation movements. Despite the stated benefits of these movements, there are some drawbacks present. One, accreditation, it must be admitted, is a process heavily based on having policies in place to meet the promulgated standards. How deep into the organization do the effects of accreditation go? Are the policies imbedded deeply enough to change performance? Secondly, too many agencies, seeing accreditation as a project but not a process, undergo only cosmetic changes. The problems remain in place be they in training, supervision, discipline or accountability. Yes, policies as a result of accreditation are considerably better; the mere fact that they exist is for many agencies an improvement.

There are more training opportunities present in the police landscape, especially those that purport to deal with executive development and leadership. Without the strong support of organizational leaders who are galvanized by a vision of the highest levels of professionalism and who stand first and foremost as an exemplar of their organizational values, the extent of change needed will not take place. To what extent do we have that momentum in place today? The quality of basic and in-service training still leaves much to be desired. Organized training objectives and lesson plans are not the standard; neither are valid tests. For many in-service training requires attendance for the record, but questionable, true learning for the participants.

However, we still bemoan the quality of supervision, especially at the first level; and again it must be said we ignore the critical importance of the supervisory role of the second level. Accountability through quality administrative investigations is far from the norm. All the while there are portents that this area will be an increasingly critical target for plaintiffs because of the statistical base it offers upon extensive reviews and analyses. In a world replete with the gathering and analysis of data, policing does not do anything close to what it should be doing to achieve sound management.

G. Patrick Gallagher

The emergence of the insurance and risk management pools

There was a time - say thirty to thirty-five years ago - when police departments went out on the open market and purchased their own insurance, searching for the best rates as a person would for auto insurance. The science of risk management was just about unknown to them. Then some police agencies started to take some heavy hits, big time judgments that attracted a lot of notice. Insurance providers realized that every department, even the smallest carried the potential for that catastrophic judgment.

When insurance company analysts projected how much they could lose by continuing to offer insurance to police, the figures were astronomical. On the chance that some convergence of all these possible losses might be bunched together, one company at a time decided to drop any coverage for police. They reasoned they could go out of business with a couple of major losses. For the few companies that stayed in the marketplace, the costs quoted for police departments spiraled upward at dizzying rates, way more than any department could afford. But where were these police departments to get coverage?

Most smaller cities belonged to statewide municipal leagues, membership organizations offering at that time some comparatively small benefits to these cities but at that time with little interaction with the police agencies of their members. Recognizing the plight of their member cities, these municipal and county leagues went to the insurance companies and asked whether or not they could get insurance if most of their members signed up for it. The insurance companies would not have to bother having insurance salesmen contact every small city for the pool formed by the municipal league would walk in the door with fifty or a hundred cities desperate for coverage. The insurance companies immediately saw their advantage: they could drastically reduce costs for marketing and selling their policies, while using the savings to reduce premiums to the municipal leagues' members.

Moreover the municipal and county leagues might create sufficient pressure to reduce the potential for losses. Some pools aggregated the members' contributions to self- insure, to pay from their accumulated funds losses up to a certain level, purchasing available reinsurance for losses over say $500,000.

Still other groups of cities and smaller jurisdictions started their own pools within states on a regional basis, paralleling the actions taken by the larger state-wide pools. Of course all these pools were not just covering police but the full range of insurance for all municipal activities: public works, fire, buildings along with professional insurance to cover local officials.

Once the municipal and county leagues entered the arena to negotiate with the insurance companies for reduced rates for their members or to provide some insurance coverage themselves, they became more insurance savvy. In effect they started their own insurance companies charging their members an appropriate fee to cover losses and simultaneously amassing some additional "rainy day" funds. Eventually they covered their losses by paying out the money sustained in judgments or settlements. The pools might require their members to retain the first $100,000 or $200,000 deductible of any loss while paying out the amount over that. They could protect themselves from the catastrophic loss by the purchase of re-insurance to cover the losses over say $500,000 or $1,000,000.

With time they realized as astute business professionals they could use the funds accumulated through the payment of premiums to further diminish losses by providing services to their police department members targeted on those problems that experience had shown them to be the most serious, such as uses of force and pursuits. They quickly became proponents of offering assistance in the development of policies; they funded all or a certain percentage of national and state accreditation. Some pools required their police department members to adopt uniform policies on certain high risk tasks, offering a discount in the insurance rates for those that adopted them. Many pools provided training on critical incident management, and general supervisory and management training.

Not every municipal league followed this pattern, however. During the course of my work I have been involved with over forty pools with some states having multiple pools like Washington and other states like Tennessee and Texas having pools that encompassed most if not all of the cities in their states.

Larger cities for the most part after the insurance crisis decided to be self-insured, setting aside funds each year in their regular budget to cover any losses. In tight urban budgets usually this money allocated for the payment of claims or liability losses did not allow for the allocation of any funds for the police department for additional training and the development of policies. These urban insurance and risk management departments seldom had any real influence in recommending or mandating any changes in the police department that might diminish losses or claims that might end in litigation. In some of these larger cities, they operated in an entirely discrete arena with no real connection to or influence on the police department.

I came across one urban risk management department whose staff had the authority to settle small claims that might have metastasized into major settlements. Since the risk management department had to be notified immediately of any potential incidents, (in the aftermath of a wrong address raid or a non-injury accident), a risk manager was given the authority to settle minor claims in the making. They would go to the residence, talk with the persons involved and offer them that day an immediate settlement of a few thousand dollars, remarking if they wanted to accept the arrangement that the city's representative would return in three days with the signed check. Now the approach which worked well for this city will obviously not cover every type of incident, but it would certainly lessen some of the burden of processing a full blown claim or lawsuit.

However, it was a different story for the risk management pools. In my personal experience with those forty-plus pools around the country, I have been involved in quite a variety of services all directed toward assisting their police departments to avoid liability, to help them out when they were in the throes of a suit, or after the final outcome of the litigation to have some follow-up services.

I have provided a variety of training programs on the high risk/critical tasks, organized training and development sessions for supervisors, managers, and executives, and addressed the topic of leadership, strategic planning and organizational climate. I have frequently reviewed policy and procedures manuals, developed model policies on the high risk/critical tasks, conducted risk assessments and brought in a team to conduct a comprehensive management study of an entire department. In the wake of a massive judgment of close to a million dollars, one pool was concerned about the ongoing membership of a particular city. After a risk assessment I could confidently state that it was a well-managed department that had an unfortunate incident happen.

A different story: Quartzsite, AZ.

Quartzsite's story goes in the opposite direction, for after an excessive string of claims and lawsuits the Arizona Municipal Risk Retention Pool (AMRRP) after repeated warning to town officials was forced to sever its relationship with the city, dropping all of its insurance coverage as of January 1, 2013.

In the preceding months the town scrambled for some type of coverage; the staff contacted nineteen insurance companies, seventeen of whom when they had examined the claims history refused to make submit any proposals. Two of them were willing to take the risk but at a much higher rates. How much higher?

Well, the insurance coverage through the AMRRP was $130,000 in annual premiums with a $2500 deductible. On the open market, the total annual premium rose to $310,000 with a deductible of $100,000. That's a 230% increase for the coverage and a deductible forty times higher than with the pool. Another bit of bad news: the AMRRP covered all the costs of legal defense, but now the town has to foot the bill for defense attorneys and all attendant expenses.

In a two-year period, Quartzsite was involved in thirty claims with possibly some still in the offing. While the greater majority resulted "from factional disputes by the Town Council and resulting employment decisions," one news article mentioned that "arrests were made by law enforcement at the direct request of town management."

Quartzsite is an extreme example. But short of termination of coverage by a pool, the October 2012 warning letter to the town officials listed a series of alternatives that AMRRP or possibly any other pool could initiate. These alternatives are as follows:

1. additional and larger deductibles on some or all lines of coverage such that the town would pay a greater share of each claim,

2. restricted insurance limits on some or all lines of coverage such as $1 million for each wrongful act where the pool's current coverage is $2 million per act,
3. reduced aggregate insurance limits on some or all lines of coverage, such as a maximum cap of $2 million paid by the pool for any or all losses by the town,
4. inclusion of defense costs inside coverage limits offered to the town by the pool which currently pays defense costs in addition to damages,
5. elimination of any excess coverage offered to the town putting the town at direct risk for any claim amounts above the pool's limits.

Citing the danger to the pool itself as a result of Quartzsite's actions, the AMRRP stated that the number of claims made by the town had created a serious financial drain on resources contributed to the pool by other Arizona towns and cities. Therefore the termination of the insurance coverage was a necessity.

I believe that more pools should take action, if they are interested in further reducing the number of claims and the amount of settlements or judgments. Not necessarily the drastic steps taken by the AMRRP but the adjustment of the amounts of deductibles, the inclusion of defense costs in the coverage limits, and increases in the costs of coverage must come into play. Additionally the pools must mandate certain changes such as improved policies, additional training, and some form of risk assessments after payout.

Would the AMRRP have been in a better position if six months, rather than two years into Quartzsite's catastrophic problems, it had mandated some form of assistance to address the factional disputes and employment issues? I think so.

Seeing the results: a case study

Do these steps pay off you might ask? Definitely they do. But can we document any real savings from a reduction in liability?

Sure it's dated, going back a little over twenty years, but there is some hard proof available in what the Missouri Intergovernmental Risk Management Association (MIRMA) and its sixty-three police departments accomplished.

With the provision of liability management and supervisory training in multiple sessions, policy development and mandatory adoption for High Risk/Critical Tasks policies, training on those HR/CTs with the highest losses or most suits, and leadership development, there was a distinct paradigm shift.

The MIRMA staff and the police chiefs realized that good leadership and management coupled with attainable high standards of performance made for healthy departments that were less prone to become involved in incidents where liability was generated. The driving forces had shifted from the mere avoidance of liability to better led, better run departments with clear cut accountability. The beast had been somewhat tamed!

What were the results in the numbers? From the figures provided by MIRMA, in a five-year period losses from police-involved activities dropped from $1,056,943 to $96, 319. Or put differently the cost per officer in the pool plummeted from $798 to $76.44. Police claims as a part of total claims down from 6.33% to 4.78%. Police claims as a percent of total losses down from 24% to 2.4%. MIRMA calculated savings in three years, 1989-1991 inclusive as $297,000, $328,000 and $381,000. The rather dramatic commitment to these programs was occasioned by heavy losses in the years preceding the aggressive provision of assistance. There was one loss in 1986 for $312,000 and eight in 1987 for $100,000 to $242,000.

While not directly producing data poolwide in 2002 the Tennessee Municipal League Risk Management Pool examined accredited and non-accredited departments looking at law enforcement liability. Non-accredited departments experienced a rate of 2.2 claims per 100 insured officers; accredited agencies were less than half that at 1.1 per hundred. Liability losses for the non-accredited agencies was $35,000 per 100 officers while the accredited agencies' losses were at $30,400 per 100 officers. Auto liability was down 31% for the accredited departments. The TML Risk Management Pool concluded that their work in providing supervisory training and encouraging police agencies to adopt standardized practices and policies through accreditation was a cost-effective investment of time and resources. The pool subsidized the Commission on Accreditation for Law Enforcement Agencies process for those agencies willing to commit to this process.

Risk assessments

Having conducted numerous risk assessments, I want to say something about the process. A risk assessment should be seen as comparable to a person's comprehensive medical examination whose purpose is to identify health problems before they become worse and to suggest any necessary steps to improve physical wellbeing and health. It is the same for the application of this process to a police department: review certain symptoms, complete an examination, diagnose, prescribe remedies, and implement them.

I have believed for many years that some form of retrospective process must be an integral part of the management of any police department. Yet we do not get the benefits from a critical examination of how the organization is performing. Lawsuits start the process in an indirect manner, but we usually do not carry it through to the conclusion where we develop the necessary action steps that will require the steps for improvement. Until we incorporate some form of this process, perhaps annually or in the aftermath of litigation we will deprive ourselves of critically valuable information and data.

In a January 2014 article "Measuring Law Enforcement Performance" (www.fbinaa.org) Dr. Jeffrey Phillips lays out the case for the:

> "value in assessing police organizations' internal controls and how that practice may assist in mitigating exposure that is inherent within police operations. By having a law enforcement performance auditing practice as part of a risk management program, law enforcement agencies may measure whether they are following their own policies and procedures, or whether such policies and procedures are adequate as internal controls to address the inherent risks of their law enforcement operations. In addition such practice may enhance the ability to mitigate their risk exposure with lawsuits."

Dr. Phillips, currently associated with the Los Angeles Police Department, quotes the U.S. Government Accountability Office's definition that:

> "audits provide findings or conclusions based on an evaluation of sufficient, appropriate evidence against set criteria. Performance audits provide objective analysis to assist management and those charged with governance and oversight in using the information to improve program

performance and operations, reduce costs, facilitate decision making by parties with responsibility to oversee or initiate correction action, and contribute to public accountability."

Even if the comprehensive audit is beyond the capabilities of the agency, at certain times in their existence, organizations like police departments can profit from an examination with varying degrees of effort of their operations, or of a particular function, along with the complete range of the necessary administrative support of those operations.

The process could be summarized in the application of the Six Layered Liability Protection System (SLLIPS) to this department or function which would include examining the policies, essential training, the quality of supervision, corrective action or discipline, a review of all pertinent data, records and required revisions, and relevant legal training and support.

I have developed a Police Audit and Risk Assessment (PARA), a comprehensive survey/questionnaire of various operational and administrative practices. It is a critical component of the total risks assessment package. The PARA asks the probing questions and gives a definite insight into the agency, thereby setting the stage for the remainder of the risk assessment and the development of recommendations for change.

There are different periods when a risk assessment can be particularly beneficial. They are when:

1. a police department is performing quite well yet wants to be informed by an objective, outside party if there are any major steps that they could take to bring their performance to an even higher level.
2. a police department has sustained a major suit leading to a substantial judgment/settlement against the department. Occasionally if this is proposed as part of a settlement, the opposing party might agree to a lesser figure in the settlement process, because they are committed strongly to affecting organizational change or the elimination of a problem or perceived abuse.
3. a police department has sustained a number of similar lawsuits e.g. uses of force, and the department or the insurer is concerned about the possibility of more in the future. The PARA might be narrowly

focused on the policies, training, quality of supervision, discipline and/or remediation, review and revision of all performance data, and legal training on that subject.
4. a police department has sustained a variety of lawsuits on different topics where there is concern about additional ones forming more serious claims for "policy and practice" thereby raising the risks and the municipal exposure considerably.
5. a police department has a particular function which has raised concern or which is an actual or expected part of litigation where it is necessary to survey all pertinent data and records to establish benchmark performance against established professional standards. This type of assessment might be centered on training, uses of force, or more commonly Internal Affairs along with the complaint acceptance and investigatory process of the department. This is especially necessary when a large amount of records and files has been turned over to opposing counsel through the process of discovery and production of documents
6. a police department or the political entity is undergoing a transition in leadership and there is a perceived need to establish baseline performance data for comparison with a soon-to-be developed strategic plan to include performance goals and objectives.

Prior to the initiation of any risk assessment, through a meeting of our staff and the entity requesting the PARA the exact parameters and scope of work will be determined to include the timetable and the form and focus of the entire process.

For local circumstances when there is current litigation in progress or it is seen as forthcoming, it is recommended that arrangements be worked out with defense counsel so that resulting reports can be seen as a work product for that attorney.

Our first step is to explain that the only objective of the process is to evade liability, to assist the department in avoiding the stress of another lawsuit. The second step is to realize that the focus has to remain on dealing with the quality of performance.

How did we go about the risk assessment?

Initially the police chief is told we are present to help him/her and the entire department avoid future organizational trauma, an experience they might have experienced in the recent past. I would first have the chief executive fill out our customized survey instrument, the Police Audit and Risk Assessment (PARA) and attach a couple of specific policies to it.

Additionally we asked the managers to respond to some questions describing the best characteristics of the department and also those that needed changing. An organizational survey would go out to all officers. When we arrived on site, we had all this information to start interviewing officers and supervisors. Finally we reviewed the major management responsibilities for the upper echelons of the department. The final report was presented with a list of recommendations for every aspect of the department so that its executive and command staff would have a clear picture of what must be implemented or changed to reduce the potential for liability while improving the overall management of the department. Usually we found quite naturally that the Six Layers of Liability Protection formed a ready template to address the issues.

I have conducted risk assessments on departments that have just taken that big hit, or ones where it is apparent that one will occur. Finally I have done the same on some excellent agencies in the different pools to see what they were doing and what made them outstanding. Policing for the most part does not engage in the process of inspections or audits, reviewing the manner in which certain functions were carried out. But an assessment, audit or review can be likened to that physical fitness examination, so that we find out who is really performing superbly, what can be improved and what should be changed as the department continues to evolve.

But back to the pools

The pools can target for training or for policy changes topics identified in their list of filed lawsuits, taking a solid lesson from settlements or judgments. Also an advisory council of police chiefs can scan the law enforcement environment and point out the necessary topics and tasks that merit the attention of the pool and its members.

It goes without saying that if there is going to be a payout, we should squeeze every lesson out of it, and get as much as possible for that expense. That means that in the aftermath of any settlement or judgment the pool should convene a meeting to examine the scope of the lawsuit and select any learning points for the pools' members.

The pools can apply a certain encouragement - or even pressure- from their board to those members who are slow or reluctant to improve policies or even have their officers attend training sessions. Some pools will offer incentives: if officers attend all training, if the department adopts the model policies developed and propagated by the pool, if they achieve state or national accreditation, the pool might refund a percentage of the city's insurance premium.

The evolving role of the pools

There is no denying the beneficial results of the pools. However, it is my observation that having satisfied that initial need for insurance coverage, many of the pools have not seen their role as providing an array of supportive activities for their members, nor have they utilized their powerful position in conjunction with their boards to establish higher standards for their members with the enhanced objective of further reducing the potential for liability.

Undoubtedly law enforcement is the better because of the pools. My point is that they could do even more to further protect their members and increase their corporate effectiveness, a lot more. I think the pools can exert a strong influence on the performance of their members, and selectively establish parameters for the continued membership of poor-performing members in the pool itself. If the pool reaches for and accepts mandatory higher standards, it is with the specific purpose of cutting down on any losses through settlements and judgments and the attendant costs of sustaining a long defense process even if the department eventually wins the suit. Pools cannot be truly successful unless its police department members are successful creating that symbiotic relationship that is truly beneficial for the pool and the police.

Previously I have said a lot on methods of raising the level of performance, and of denying plaintiffs and their attorneys the raw material essential for a lawsuit: the allegation of lower level performance not in conformity with professional standards. It goes without saying if the performance is raised appreciably, then there will be fewer suits, the costs would decrease, individual members' contributions to the pool will be lowered, and more funds might be available to provide training and support services for the departments.

How is this success achieved through the efforts of the insurance and risk management pools? Here are some suggestions. Since as we have seen performance is affected proactively, actively and reactively I will propose them in that order.

Proactive phase suggestions

1. In conjunction with the pool's board set aside funds to provide critically needed services for the members. (One pool in the Western U.S. purchased a discretionary shooting simulator and moved it from one department to another to guarantee that this activity was covered because the chiefs had identified the need.)
2. Again in conjunction with the board consider providing assistance for each member to achieve national accreditation through the Commission on Accreditation for Law Enforcement Agencies (CALEA) or through the parallel state process for accreditation. The achievement of accreditation could occasion some decrease in the agency's cost of insurance coverage.
3. For those agencies who do not go for accreditation provide assistance through workshops and training on the topics relating to the twelve High Risk/Critical Tasks. Develop model policies for these 12 tasks and then require that all these members adopt and promulgate these policies to their officers. If the agency does not want to adopt the model policy then it must show that its policies' components are equivalent to the model policy.
4. Establish an advisory board of police chiefs to alert the pool to specific problems employing them to discuss pertinent issues and to serve the pool by disseminating messages to the other chiefs. Have the advisory board assist the pool in devising an annual strategic plan listing areas of focus. Discuss with them and the pool's board methods for tightening up the management and oversight of claims and lawsuits. Develop higher standards for membership in the pool

while discussing the means of dealing with those agencies that are making excessive demands on the pool's resources. This should include the process for dropping an agency from membership.
5. Establish certain requirements for the training of all supervisors and provide assistance to get them trained.
6. Assist in the procurement of computerized employee performance management software similar to Guardian Tracking along with a methodology for policy management, policy training and testing similar to Power DMS. (This does not constitute an endorsement of these systems, but they are quite widely used satisfactorily by many police agencies.)

Active phase suggestions

7. Collect data on HR/CT incidents from members to determine when the pool as a whole or a group of member agencies needs some extra scrutiny or assistance.
8. Calculate clearly the cost per dollar of income to support the police function in the aggregate for the entire pool, then break that cost down for each member. Answer the question, agency by agency of the cost per officer of providing the coverage and services. There may be some way of rewarding those agencies that have drastically reduced costs to the pool by lowering their premiums. Obviously as a result of successfully defending a department a member's cost for one year or two might escalate considerably.
9. Constantly track on other data annually such as the percentage increase in the cost to the pool for each department in payments, settlements and legal defense; for an officer in each department, for claims per department and each officer, police claims as a percentage of all claims in the pool, and the loss ratio (cost per dollar of income paid out in claims, judgments) increase or decrease for each department and for the pool in general. Also track on the number of vehicle accidents, the number of pursuits, the number of serious uses of force contrasted to the number of complaints and lawsuits using these data to determine training initiatives.
10. Continuously provide selected training programs.

Reactive phase suggestions

11. Require each member to alert the pool when an event happens that might end up in a lawsuit. As other pools have done, assess whether or not there is a chance to settle the claim in a timely manner.
12. When a suit is filed, have the defense counsel meet with the pool officials and the chief to devise a strategy for the case.
13. As the suit progresses have the defense counsel meet with the chief and the pool officials to suggest steps which should be taken immediately to improve the department's performance. Include information from the reviews of the expert witnesses for the same purpose.
14. When the suit is settled or comes to judgment, convene a meeting with the defense counsel to develop recommendations to place the department in a stronger position in the future.
15. After the culmination of the suit, whether through settlement or judgment, require that that department go through a risk or liability assessment with the purpose of bringing to the surface any other areas which need attention. (This would be equivalent to a physical examination after a medical problem.)
16. Have the pool's board take a strong stand on agencies that will not make changes as a result of the risk assessment. If the agency is involved in several lawsuits, then the risk assessment might have to provide recommendations as to whether that agency should remain in the pool. Every pool seems to have at least one agency that shows little attention to basic liability prevention. Rather than letting the rest of the pool carry this member, conduct a risk assessment, develop a timeline for improvement based on the recommendations and in the absence of improvement, place it on probation, increase its payment to the pool, and/or as an alternative, sever its membership from the pool.
17. Through a demanding selection process, choose one or two members of the pool who are willing to engage in a comprehensive risk management program that might start at vehicle damage and crashes, seat belt usage and go to a continuum of many of the suggestions in this book and others that can be devised. Monitor these agencies over time to find connections between the various

programs and upgrades. In effect lavish some resources on these agencies. Assess what the results turn out to be.
18. Include these figures in the annual report for the pool.

An expanded role for the chief of police

I think our present situation *vis a vis* liability is partially attributable to the more narrow role of police management, one that does not contain risk management as part of that responsibility. While the police are necessarily involved in the action which initiates the litigation, there is a disconnect that occurs. Quite soon after the initiation of any legal action the department becomes more distant from the process that ends in a trial. This disconnect becomes more distant from the legal process that ends in the trial.

When a suit is filed, the city attorney's office or the insurance pool is notified. After that notification attorneys vetted and hired by the city (in some cases the attorneys might be on the staff of the municipality) or the pool enter the arena becoming the agency's defenders. The process is entirely controlled outside of the agency; few chiefs play any role unless they have to appear for a deposition, and if named in the suit, sit through the trial.

To me there is a necessity to revise the management responsibilities of the executive to include an all-encompassing function of risk management. I say that the chief should always meet with the selected defense attorneys early on and at other critical points during the run-up to the depositions and the trial, hearing their feedback on the case as it develops, asking them for recommendations.

This information should be used immediately to start the changes so that there is less chance that a similar situation will expose the department to another suit. Minimally this is needed to guarantee that the department is in a much stronger position if it were to face similar incidents. That is the time to start changing or updating policy, to improving training, getting a special message out to supervisors and highlighting the points of concern.

If there are problems, why wait two or three years until the lawsuit is settled? Some departments will not even initiate the investigation of the complaint accompanying a filed lawsuit until that distant day when the suit is settled.

Here is the danger as I see it. Suppose the suit was based on a complaint of excessive force or sexual misconduct. If the department does nothing, puts aside the complaint and waits for the conclusion of the suit, suppose a year later another similar incident generates lawsuit #2; according to practice the department does nothing. Just to push this example a little further, yet suppose nine months later another similar incident occurs.

Now let's say the plaintiff's attorneys in lawsuit #3 in the request for production of documents sweep up all the documents for lawsuits 1, 2 and 3. The department has done nothing to further the investigation of the complaint; there is no internal action tied to the subject matter of the complaints and therefore its stance could be construed as a "custom or practice" of condoning this conduct (as it will undoubtedly be argued by the plaintiff's attorney). There is no question but the department's potential exposure makes it more glaringly vulnerable to a much heavier judgment.

On the other hand, if the department from the time the executive hears about the concerns of the attorneys, takes steps to alleviate the problem by policy changes and improvements in training, those steps will stand out in its favor, the agency is in a better light, and the outcome's chances are most likely to be a more favorable outcome.

Aside from the conferencing with the defense attorneys early in the case about substantive issues, the chief should make sure that the involved officers have gone over their incident reports, the relevant policies, their training records and their contents. You might say that these points are no-brainers. When queried by the plaintiff's attorney about what the officer had gone over to prepare for the deposition, there is the occasional glaring omission that nothing was reviewed. You only have to read through numerous deposition transcripts to hear the constant refrain of "I don't know," "I may have been given that policy," "I don't know whether we have one," and "I may have seen that once before." These comments do not strengthen the case for the defense.

Actually a checklist should be established for every case and all those who are to eventually be deposed should be familiar with every item which it contains. The chief or someone in the department should make sure that these documents and records are reviewed. The chief could even sit in on the depositions to glean any other information as to methods for immediately strengthening the department's defenses.

In a larger department, at least for the few that have a risk management unit or function in staff services or professional standards, the unit manager might be delegated to develop memos to the chief executive for recommended changes.

We have to face the reality that risk management as it relates proactively, actively and reactively to the reality of litigation and the active involvement of generally accepted risk management concepts is hardly present at all. If it is present, the units do not have the status and input that they need to be able to share their insights and data with the other administrative divisions in the department.

These steps are not new to policing but they are applied in other contexts of crime prevention, crime investigation, administrative guidance and operational implementation of new programs with assessments of their effectiveness. Now, front and center, they have to be developed into management protocols for every department. Risk management and its attendant processes must be integrated into the comprehensive management of every police department. The results will speak for themselves.

CHAPTER 15

MOVING FORWARD: SUGGESTIONS FOR THE ROAD AHEAD

"Police departments must worship at the altar of high level performance. They must remember that policies, training, supervision, and discipline are merely inputs to achieve that. The only acceptable output is high level performance."

-Gallagher's Principles #16

"The Primary Person Principle requires the leader to have a vision, to stand for and develop values, and to affect the culture of the organization."

-Tom Peters

"For true quality and high level performance we have to gather and analyze data. Secondly we have to realize that before we have people problems we have process problems. Finally we have to instill joy in the workplace."

-Edwards Deming

As a profession we must think of the future, and devise the particular steps which can be taken to enhance the profession to which so many dedicated men and women have devoted their lives, and many literally given their lives.

A number of years ago I was listening to the then-chief of the Prince Georges County (MD) Police Department bemoan the difficulty he was experiencing in inaugurating new programs in the agency. There were plenty of solid obstacles in getting people to go along with his change agenda, let alone getting them to embrace it.

I said to the chief: "Chief, have you ever looked at the motto on your shoulder patch?" He responded with: "Sure, but there's some Latin motto and I have no idea what it means." I said: "The motto is *'Semper eadem'* which means 'Always the same.' I think you should change the motto first and then see if you can change the department." Choosing this motto of the former Queen Elizabeth I from over four hundred years ago probably had some merit when it was first selected, but now it might just be an impediment to the updating desperately needed in the agency.

Whether it's official or not, some professions, some organizations and some managers are unconsciously committed to this motto, for they want to stay in the same place, not realizing the critical need for change and updating.

How many times do we get notices from our tech provider that our operating system is to be updated? Disregarding the notice we can embrace the status quo, but to extract the best from our system we proceed with the update. We take it for granted that somewhere out there in cyberspace at the end of these technological tendrils I.T. experts have been working to improve the system and downloading those changes will allow us to work more smoothly, more efficiently.

In these our times, the message is clear that over and above our computer capability there are any number of factors that need updating: our management styles, our organizations, our ideas and certainly our knowledge. Thus it is with risk management for policing must evolve more to incorporate the techniques of that discipline and apply it to every facet of our operations.

You know we all have goals, we make promises as at New Year's but like those resolutions the goal has to be concretized, with specific action steps. With the overarching reasons for reducing liability through performance at the highest levels I feel that the police profession must unite behind some processes that to me will undoubtedly help to achieve that end.

If you have been with me through the preceding chapters, you can certainly glean a number of ideas. But here are some other suggestions for consideration to improve the profession.

If risk management concepts were to drive police performance there will be two solid effects: liability will be decreased and organizational professionalism will be increased.

But we have to face the reality that risk management as it relates proactively, actively and reactively to the reality of litigation is hardly present at all. We have not heeded the clear warnings and illustrations of incipient problems. The time has come to listen if only to make the job easier for ourselves Make personnel conscious of risk management principles just as much as they are conscious of officer safety.

At risk of being too repetitious (I will admit I have been to reinforce key concepts) I will bring these thoughts together with a few final recommendations.

Training of supervisors

I consider the role of first line supervisors so important that I don't think anyone should be placed in this position unless he/she has been trained sufficiently to become the quality control inspector for all performance.

I believe that as part of the training, there should be some form of Field Training Supervisor program to introduce the newly minted but still on probation first line supervisors to the full gamut of their responsibilities.

I believe that second line supervisors should be tasked with developing, nurturing and supporting the role of the first line supervisors and that this task should be the one that is made a number one priority.

I believe that second line supervisors should undergo a course enabling them to better perform this critical task, their primary task.

The training of both first and second line supervisors must include a series of scenarios that will teach and test them on their ability to handle the various tasks inherent in the position.

Decertification of officers

I believe that once officers show that they are not fulfilling the obligations and responsibilities of their positions, or even more seriously not living up to the requirements of their oaths of office, and are found to have serious sustained charges against them or are guilty of criminal charges, there should be a review by a state agency for decertification. (Conviction of a criminal offense might become grounds for an automatic revocation of a person's certification.) There should be some connection between the pre-employment standards which allowed them to get into the profession and their failure to maintain those standards. Then they should be ushered out of the profession for they are not worthy to carry the badge.

Florida's **Professional Compliance Process** available from the bureau chief in charge of standards for the Florida Department of Law Enforcement basically requires all major criminal and administrative charges to be sent on to Tallahassee for follow-up investigation. Revocation is mandatory for most felonies and for some misdemeanors (pleading guilty to perjury or false statements). Conviction at trial is not necessary for if an officer pleads guilty or nolo contendere regardless of a withholding of adjudication or suspension of sentence that suffices for decertification. Decertification occurs also for failure to maintain "good moral character." Finally non-criminal acts such as excessive use of force, misuse of official position as in sexual harassment involving physical contact, sex while on duty, subverting the state approved examination process, and willful failure of an agency administrator to comply with the state statutes as they pertain to the Criminal Justice Standards and Training Commission rules can also bring about decertification.

I believe that every state should require the police executive in the light of certain levels of serious administrative charges and/or criminal charges to have those files forwarded to a state agency for review for possible decertification.

Along these lines I believe that internal investigations should not be aborted without coming to a conclusion even if officers who realize that the department can make a case against them, decide to suddenly resign. They look for another agency; these "gypsy" cops should not be allowed to move from one agency to another. Internal investigations to the extent possible should be completed.

The profession deals with evidence constantly. There is plenty of evidence amassed about certain officers through complaints and lawsuits, serious conduct unbecoming an officer (CUBO), or criminal charges and subsequent convictions that proclaim these persons should not remain in their positions of trust. They, by their actions, are lowering the public's opinion of policing. They are not thinking of the thousands of officers committed to serving with distinction, honesty, and probity. Those offenders should not remain in the profession.

Greater frequency of individual and unit reviews and audits

The profession has to renew and expand the practice of conducting reviews and audits of performance to learn what could be done better, to catalog what should be eliminated as a practice or initiated as policy and training. These audits and reviews should be positively critical, pointing out the shortcomings so that there can be organizational learning taking place. We will get nothing from *pro forma* reviews that refrain from saying anything negative, that highlight no problems, that outline recommendations that are neither discussed nor evaluated, and certainly not implemented. When it comes to avoiding the organizational trauma of more litigation the recommendations of the review or audit process forming a type of action plan can contribute to the strengthening of the department's defenses from liability. These reviews might be initiated and supported by the insurance or risk management pool as part and parcel of their services to their members. Review team members could even be from another department so that the process would contribute to their managerial sophistication.

Consolidation of police departments

Cities, towns and villages do not want to surrender their right to have their own police departments, but we have to admit to the vast duplication in facilities and manpower. The argument is voiced that larger departments can provide more specialized services. This is not the ultimate panacea. Yes, the topic is highly controversial. There is some consolidation going on but the concept frankly has never been popular. Regional police forces do exist. Some almost in my area are forming and one is dissolving. Residents in small municipalities want the dedicated service of their departments and are not clamoring to hand it on to some other entity geographically removed from their locations.

Local officials tend to like the idea of having a certain control, input and possible influence over their agencies. But at some point, because of the financial crunch the resources to support these forces might not remain available and consolidation might be talked about. Admittedly while there is this attachment to the local police, there are certain tasks that they would find challenging: the necessary training, the full policy direction and adequate supervision. While consolidation might not come, the multiplicity of smaller departments which represent the norm in American policing must upgrade their administration and operations otherwise the stray lawsuit might devastate them.

The police culture and liability

Collectively and individually there are vast quantities of resources poured into bettering the profession's chances of avoiding liability. But the discussion of the varying effectiveness of each contribution must be considered in the light of the police culture itself.

For years I have been querying police training sessions asking them this question. What contributes the most to the quality of the performance of new officers?
Is it –

- Their personal culture, their upbringing, education, and/or religion?
- The popular culture of policing as portrayed in the media such as TV and movies?
- The quality of their basic academy training?
- The department's mission, vision and corporate values?
- The Field Training Officer (FTO) program?
- The departmental culture, the manner and style of the veteran officers as seen by the new officers?

Invariably without exception the immediate response has been the last one, - the departmental culture. In further discussions with the training session's participants, we agreed that if the veteran officers were doing everything correctly then this period would solidify what preceded it in their previous training. But is that the case? Once again there was agreement that a lot of what was going on in the street was possibly contrary or not in conformity to training and policies. But as Edwin J. Delattre points out in **Character and Cops: Ethics in Policing** new officers "conform externally in order to be accepted internally." Policing is not possible if an officer is not sure where he stands in relationship to the officers who might be coming to his aid in critical situations. That external acceptance is not to be gained by imitating all of other officers' actions.

Since these comments focus on street performance, the police culture and acceptance by fellow officers play a crucial part that heavily influences performance, and certainly possible liability.

These questions could be raised: "Can we really combat or lessen liability in the face of the police culture? Could we accomplish this feat without the support of the police culture? What would it take to influence that culture? How do you as a chief taking over a department effect this change?" It all goes to say that the culture's influence for better or worse has to be addressed.

Again, and finally the Leadership Test

The Gallagher-Westfall Group historically has proposed that the Leadership Test be employed to guide our decisions. It reads as follows:

> **Am I doing:**
>   **The right thing?**
>   **In the right way?**
>   **At the right time?**
>   **For the right reason?**

If every executive, every supervisor, every officer were to submit actions and decisions to this test and allow it to guide their actions then an uplift in performance both individually and organizationally cannot but be present. Liability will be managed; it will be decreased.

APPENDIX A

A Response to Chapter 9, "Viewing Police Performance from the Other Side"

In Chapter Nine, you were asked to review a set of facts relating to an actual police incident summarized in those pages. You were then asked to view the facts of the incident as a potential expert witness for the plaintiff's case to see what, in the light of these circumstances, might be suggested as points for the plaintiff's side.

You were asked to view the police response as objectively as possible, setting aside a very natural tendency to side with fellow officers. The purpose is to see and examine the process. However, it is critical that we in evaluating the actions of police, if we expect to decrease the negative impact of liability, apply professional standards and make honest judgments with the intention of performing at the highest levels.

True, you don't have access to all the documents, but what is summarized below will give you an idea of the research that might be marshaled to support the plaintiff's case. In what follows I will offer some ideas on the points as the plaintiffs' case is established, the issues from an expert's perspective that must be discussed, and which then could become eventually the bases for the opinions.

(Note: In training sessions I usually give out only a partial summary, outlining the incident faced by the sheriff's department's supervisor and three deputies up to the point where they are on site and are told by the son what is the situation in the back yard. Divided into groups they are asked to outline a plan for dealing with the circumstances surrounding the conduct of Mr. Gordon. Invariably the response entails a rather solid and professional plan. Finally I will share with them the actual reaction of the sheriff's contingent. Having already outlined their response, many are reluctant to take a strong stand in their role as a plaintiff's expert since it might be interpreted as criticism of those officers. However, we must be critical in a positive sense to learn as much as we can from performance that departs from accepted standards.

To initiate this process, I would propose we look at five individual issues and attempt to develop opinions for them. The questions to be raised are:

1. Did the policies meet national and generally accepted performance standards for dealing with the mentally ill, those with diminished capacity, or those with suicidal tendencies?
2. Was the deputies' training under this sheriff adequate and up to national standards for use of force, critical incident response and dealing with the mentally ill, those with diminished capacity or those with suicidal tendencies?
3. Had the subject committed any offense? Was the taser's use immediately upon the deputies' entry into the yard before the subject made any movement a legitimate use of force?
4. Was the use of deadly force against the subject objectively reasonable?
5. Did the department follow its own policies?

Finally we must address what would be the proper approach to this incident.

The Response

The issues are:

1. Did the policies of this department meet the generally accepted performance standards for police agencies for dealing with the mentally ill and those with suicidal tendencies?

For the past two decades or more there has been a growing awareness of the need for special policies and training and even specially certified officers to deal with the mentally ill and those with suicidal tendencies.

Developments in something of a chronological order included the formation in a large county of a Mobile Crisis Unit in the early 1980s. Then the Police Executive Research Forum (PERF) published in 1986 **Improving the Police Response to the Mentally Disabled** which laid out the steps officers should take when dealing with the mentally ill and those with suicidal intentions.

This publication's purposes were to guide the development of policy and procedures that must be in place. Additionally it makes recommendations for basic and in-service training such as the following:

1. Evaluation of the situation before taking action and developing written procedures which should include:
    - the officers' responsibilities in handling an encounter to determine whether the person is mentally ill or dangerous,
    - determining whether a violation of the law has occurred,
    - determining the appropriate disposition, and accomplishing these tasks while ensuring that no harm comes to the subject, any bystanders, or the officer;
2. If the subject is suicidal, contact supervisors or special units, wait for assistance, and establish communications;
3. Officers should not rush or attempt to overpower the person unless someone's safety is threatened;
4. If subject is acting dangerously but not directly threatening any other person or himself, let him calm down for "time is the officer's ally;"
5. Taking an adversarial approach will worsen the situation. "Tough methods will usually frighten the person and cause him or her to react in a defensive or possible violent manner;"
6. Only when a person is so dangerous or violent that himself or another is likely to be harmed should force be used.

In 1997 PERF published another book, **The Police Response to People with Mental Illness** which addressed more of the training issues in a series of modules and is an expansion of the previous work with more emphasis as mentioned on training officers along with a model policy for all departments.

In a module recommending approaches to those with mental illness, officers are cautioned to:

1. remain calm and avoid overreacting,
2. announce actions before taking them,
3. gather information from family and bystanders, and
4. have someone from a local health organization respond to the scene.

Actions to be avoided include: moving suddenly, giving rapid orders or shouting, crowding the person or moving into his comfort zone, and not allowing the person to calm down if they are not harming anyone.

One major message is "communication is essential to successful management," which allows the "officer to gain valuable information regarding the problem, enabling him and the subject to understand each other and in turn, reducing the tension that accompanies these encounters."

That same year the IACP brought out their model policy for dealing with the mentally ill. This policy and the expanded concept paper repeated many of the components in the PERF publications indicating there should be no threats of arrest, steps should be taken to calm the situation, officers should assume a non-threatening manner, and they should summon crisis intervention specialists to assist them.

However, it was the Memphis (TN) Police Department that in the interim between the two PERF publications that deserves the credit for the development of the most complete program in linking up with local universities and the Memphis Chapter of the Alliance for the Mentally Ill. The department organized, trained and implemented a special police unit which evolved into the Memphis Crisis Intervention Team (CIT) whose officers had taken up to twenty hours talking with persons with psychiatric disabilities. The key strategy of the Memphis CIT and other CIT groups around the country is to "slow things down."

A Center for Public Representation article summarizes the results of the Memphis CIT work by stating:

> "The results of the program include drastically lowered deaths and injuries (interestingly the rate of deaths and injuries to police officers was reduced

more than the rate of injuries to people with psychiatric disabilities but both have declined dramatically) and an arrest rate that is one tenth the national average on calls associated with psychiatric disabilities."

By now this acronym has been generalized to stand for a special group of officers in police departments called upon to deal with incidents involving the mentally ill. Police executives had certainly been placed on notice.

The CIT model has specially trained officers on every shift, offers ongoing training, and is characterized as "the necessary adjustment that law enforcement must make from a traditional police response to a more humane treatment of individuals with mental illness." It has been credited with making crisis response immediate, a diminution in uses of force, and training officers in de-escalation techniques.

Building on the Memphis Model of the CIT, the Valley Crisis Intervention Team (VCIT) Program located 50 miles from this sheriff's department, was established in 2004 through grant funds and sent its team of twenty persons to Memphis to be trained by the program's creators.

While initially focusing its efforts on the Valley, it has expanded its efforts to provide forty-hour training programs throughout the state. Through a partnership with the state Police Officers Standards and Training Commission and the founders of the Memphis Model, the VCIT has offered its resources to help other areas develop their own CITs. It has trained 48 law enforcement agencies from around the state, seventeen of which are sheriffs' departments to allow for CIT-trained officers to respond to incidents involving mental illness.

<u>Commission on Accreditation for Law Enforcement Agencies (CALEA) National Standard for Police and Mentally Ill</u>

Finally, CALEA promulgated standard 41.2.7 reading as follows:

> "The agency has a written directive regarding the interaction of agency personnel with persons suspected of suffering from mental illness that addresses:
>
> a. guidelines for the recognition of persons suffering from mental illness;

    b.   procedures for accessing available community mental health resources;
    c.   specific guidelines for sworn officers to follow in dealing with the persons they suspect are mentally ill during contacts on the street, as well as during interviews and interrogations;
    d.   documented entry level training of agency personnel; and
    e.   documented refresher training at least every two years."

Estimates of Mentally Ill Persons in Police Calls-for-Service

The pervasiveness of the problem in dealing with the mentally ill is borne out by the estimated percentage of persons with varying degrees of mental illness of between 7-10 percent. They constitute enough of the population directly served by police to warrant the special policy directives and training similar to that for other special tasks such as hostage and barricaded situations, or special populations to include developmentally handicapped, rape victims, diabetics, and abused children.

LaGrange (GA) and Bethlehem (PA) Policies on Mentally Ill

Chief Lou Dekmar of the LaGrange (GA) Police Department is currently chairperson of the eighteen member CALEA board that passes on the suitability of applicants for accreditation and chief of a CALEA-nationally accredited agency. His agency's policy, titled: "Patrol Functions: Responding to Persons with Mental Illness," shows the integration of CIT officers with patrol, and the specific and general recommendations given to all responders. Note that when the CIT officer arrives on the scene, he/she will assume the primary role in handling the call with strong statements to "use time as your ally," "avoid rushing the person," "make slow, cautious moves," and "use a low, calm voice."

The Bethlehem (PA) Police Department is both CALEA-accredited nationally and through the state process. Their policy on "Interaction with Persons Suspected of Suffering from Mental Illness," coupled with that relating to the "Crisis Intervention Team," and the "Emergency Response Team" provide for the responding officers to hand the incident over to the special teams (which also includes the Tactical Emergency Medical Service). It is to be noted that the CIT for this department is to deal with suicidal persons through the "use of verbal and psychological tactics as a primary effort."

Critical Role of Negotiators

Situations similar to this one, across the police profession, require the critical insertion of a trained negotiator who was promptly called to the scene to interact with field commanders in critical incidents. The negotiator when brought to the scene realizes that the greatest ally is time; the fast-paced blitzkrieg-like actions of SWAT teams are foreign to this person.

Agencies of the size involved in this incident if they have an active SWAT team, probably also had a negotiator available to the team who could receive additional training for these situations.

None of the policies submitted by this department through discovery includes any mention of alternative approaches to dealing with the mentally ill despite the raft of professional indicators that highlight their importance, and despite the participation of seventeen other sheriffs' departments which have trained CIT officers and established CIT teams, and despite the failure to utilize other training resources throughout the state.

The administrative guidance for this department is completely devoid of direction to its deputies to make use of any different approaches for the mentally ill and suicidal subjects. The absence of these directives clearly indicates that the sheriff was totally unaware that his deputies needed this direction. It was clearly foreseeable that they were going to have to respond not only to calls involving suicidal subjects but a whole spectrum of persons with mental illness.

2. **Was the training given to the deputies of the sheriff's office adequate and up to national standards in the areas of use of force, critical incident response and dealing with the mentally ill?**

Training in the 12 High Risk/Critical Task Policies

Mere policy dissemination, if it takes place, is not sufficient to prepare deputies to handle critical tasks. There are twelve High Risk/Critical Tasks which generate over 95% of the potential liability for law enforcement officers performing their duties. One of these is "Dealing with the mentally ill, emotionally disturbed persons or persons with diminished capacity."

As we have seen above in evaluating policy, these particular tasks are so important that they must have specially focused training on the policies and procedures relating to their performance. Officers should not only be trained in these twelve policies, but they should be "re-certified" annually in their content and application. While admittedly the department does not offer any proof of having a policy on this topic, there are also no indications from the training records that any of the deputies have been trained in the special requirements of dealing with the mentally ill.

A prime example of this point is the training record of the sergeant, the supervisor on the scene and the person responsible for the "plan" employed by the deputies on that fateful June day in 2008. Over the course of his eleven years on the department, this sergeant had 75 separate courses logged in for his training: fully one-third related to use of force.

This sergeant's records also indicate that he had eighty-five hours of SWAT training. But there is nothing related to critical incident management, crisis intervention, or dealing with the mentally ill. In 2003 he completed a forty-hour First Line Supervision Course which had no critical incident training.

The extensive production of records on firearms and force training shows no records of FATS/discretionary (shoot/don't shoot) or judgmental training, where officers are presented with various scenarios and challenged to make the correct decision as to using force at various levels. It is universally accepted that: high level performance is a combination of professional knowledge, requisite skills and superior decision making.

All the skill development, all the requalification are comparatively meaningless, if officers entrusted with their awesome powers and authority, do not combine their honed skills with weapons, along with the knowledge of the policies and their training, and have the experience to make the appropriate decisions as to when they are to use that skill, i.e. when to use basic SWAT techniques, when to rush an armed subject threatening them, or when to forego using those skills and resort to procedures directing them to take alternative approaches.

It is surprising that the department's policy on the "Use of Force," under the topic of "Privileged Force,"(also repeated in training documents) states: "Whether the force was applied in a good faith effort to maintain and restore order or maliciously for the very purpose of causing harm." The department force policy issued in 2000 makes mention of **Graham v. Connor** while still maintaining the outdated subjective test for reasonableness from the older case of **Johnson v. Glick**.

Deputies, if they followed the policy, could apply the superseded case law rather than the current one, and could justify uses of force based on "their good faith effort to maintain and restore order." The training documents presented for review also reiterate the standards of **Johnson v. Glick.**

But what is disturbing in examining the critical area of training on the use of force in the documents presented for review, is that **Johnson v. Glick** is mentioned as the standard for determining whether or not the force used is excessive. The training document states:

> "The Supreme Court applied a four part standard that became known as the objective Reasonableness Standard," which includes "whether it was applied in a good faith effort to maintain control or maliciously and sadistically for the purposes of causing harm."

This is definitely the subjective, not the objective reasonableness standard.

Deputies trained under this program with their "Use of Force" policy have to be confused when a couple of slides later in the Powerpoint, the trainer presents **Graham v. Connor** as eliminating **Johnson v. Glick**. This misinformation or confusing and contradictory information on a topic like the use of force certainly on its face is negligent especially in the sense the deficient training would relate to the two instances where major force was applied in this incident.

Furthermore, from the documents presented it is apparent that there was no training given to the deputies in dealing with the mentally ill; an oversight which is conspicuous because of the availability of training programs, and the ready use of that training by other sheriffs' offices.

3. **Was the employment of the tasers immediately upon entering the yard and even before the subject made any movement a legitimate use of force?**

The sergeant was acknowledged by the other three deputies as the person in charge, by reason of his rank. The other deputies, it is clear, listened to him as he interviewed the person at this address, made a quick evaluation of an alternative approach to the back yard and rejected it. Immediately after he discarded the method of having someone go through the house to the back yard, and he finally determined their course of action: concealing themselves behind the wooden privacy fence extending about fifteen feet from the right side of the back of the house, peeking in to see the "two females (sic) and one male" and their positions. He then devised the plan of action that they were to go in, announcing themselves, and immediately using their tasers if the subject moved.

He determined the order of the entry: himself and the three other deputies with the trainee coming in last. He assigned tasks to each of the deputies: the long gun to one, secondary deadly force to the trainee, and the second taser to other deputy. He determined the time and point of entry, and later when unsuccessful with his taser, shouted: "Gun! Shoot him!"

No one, certainly not the sergeant, in making these decisions in the most abbreviated of time periods, questioned why they were using force against a person that had up to that point committed no crime and for which they had no cause for arrest.

A review of the department's policy on the "Use of Force, Less Lethal Electro-Muscular Disruption Device (EMDD)" indicates the department's policy:

> "This policy is consistent with this agency's direction to use only that level of force necessary to control or otherwise subdue violent or potentially violent individuals. The use of this device is intended to reduce the potential injury to the subject who may be violent or resisting violently."

Further into the policy the use of the taser is restricted as follows:

> "The EMDD is considered to be a less lethal force option at the same level as OC Spray (Level 3) or Intermediate Force (Level 4) on the

Use of Force Continuum. Deputies may elect to deploy the EMDD in circumstances that meet the criteria outlined in the Sheriff's Use of Force Policy contained in G.O. 10-01."

In G.O. 10-01, "Use of Force," in I, "Policy," it states:

"The degree of force used depends on what the deputy perceives as reasonable and necessary under the circumstances. The Sheriff's Office expects that deputies will only employ that amount of force necessary to accomplish a legal purpose. The objective in use of any force of any type is to overcome the suspect's unlawful resistance to a deputy's lawful purpose. The application of this policy requires that deputies do not unreasonably or unnecessarily endanger themselves or the public."

The mention of the Use of Force Continuum in the EMDD policy begs the question: What is the Use of Force Continuum? How does it apply to the employment of the taser?

Deputies are supposed to make "every effort to comply with the Force Continuum." As described in G.O. 10-01, "Use of Force," the Continuum is a series of escalations in the various uses of force dependent on the subject's compliance, or resistance (passive or active) or actual assaultive behavior with physical injury or assaultive behavior with serious physical injury or death toward the deputy or another person. Linked to each level of subject activity is a level of justifiable force. The EMDD policy equates the use of the taser to Level 3 (OC) or Level 4 ("impact weapons, flashlights, radios or other weapons designed to temporarily disable or incapacitate a person").

Now Level 3 in the "Use of Force" policy is described as "Physical Compliance for failure to obey verbal direction or command," and is employed by the deputy through the "use of an approved aerosol control agent if a person exhibits resistance or aggression by verbal or physical means indicating non-compliance." Level 3 is also used to "force compliance by inflicting pain to specific points on the person." Finally Level 3 is utilized through "counter move techniques that impede a person's movement towards a deputy such as blocking, striking, kicking followed by appropriate controlling techniques."

By no stretch of the imagination does Mr. Gandy's action come anywhere close to exhibiting the requisite degree of "resistance" or "aggression" that would merit this Level 3 use of force. He was not given any commands so he was not disregarding them.

If Level 3 does not justify that force, the higher use of force in Level 4 certainly does not qualify for it is restricted to "failure to obey verbal commands and/or physical resistance." Equating the taser to the use of impact weapons at this level means that the same criteria should be employed for the impact weapon as the taser, i.e. primarily "used to defend the deputy or others from serious bodily injury or death or to gain control of a violent, resistant person."

By their own policies for the EMDD and the "Use of Force," the very restrictions issued by the sheriff himself in 2000 for "Force" and July of 2007 for the EMDD instruct deputies not to employ tasers for there was no resistance, there was no non-compliance, there was no aggression by Mr. Gordon against the deputies.

No Internal Affairs investigation in measuring the deputies' actions against the policy could come up with a finding of force used within policy for there was a direct policy violation. Since the deployment and use of the tasers did not meet the criteria outlined in "Use of Force" policy, the tasers by direct order of the sheriff could not legitimately be used.

Mr. Gordon was totally passive, speaking quite calmly to his wife and a neighbor, and was smoking a cigarette and drinking a beer. No reasonable officer would judge his conduct to be anywhere violent. Therefore the group led by the sergeant violated their own policy in making the entry and attempting to taser Mr. Gordon.

Led by the sergeant, the deputies were planning the use of a high level of intrusive force on a man whom they knew from radio reports to be suicidal, to have been on his medications, who had a history of seeing a psychiatrist, and at that exact time was sitting on a wall in his back yard, smoking a cigarette and having a beer. What was the crime calling on the deputies to take action? What constituted the threat level or lack of obedience to their commands at the point of entry that justified the use of this level of force?

It is interesting to note that the department's own training encourages officers to use "Verbalization," for "effective verbalization may avoid the need for force; your suspect must know what to do; verbalization is used to transfer ownership of the force decision; verbalization may buy critical time." There was no verbalization as recommended, between the sergeant and Mr. Gordon.

The lack of proper direction by the sergeant is evident when the Garrity statements and what is presumed to be the statement taken by a detective after Mirandizing the officer firing the shots. There is certainly unanimity as the deputies describe the lead role of the sergeant. The statements of the deputies are as follows:

<u>Deputy Who Used Deadly Force</u>

- "Sergeant told me they were going in the gate and tase him (Gordon) right away before he could make any movements."
- "Sergeant reiterated that we were going to go in and tase him right away and if the subject made any threatening motions to shoot him."
- "I saw Mr. Gordon sitting on the wall, taking a drag from a cigarette with his right hand. I brought my rifle up, shining the flashlight onto Gordon."
- "When the tasers went off, Gordon then threw down the cigarette and stood up, and Gordon lunged forward."
- "Gordon was running for the door, somebody yelled 'Gun' and this was immediately followed by the sergeant saying 'Shoot him.'"
- "The sergeant advised us of the plan which was …I would be covering them and that if he made any threatening movements towards us to shoot him while he and the other deputy had their tasers out."
- "As we entered I saw the man taking a draft from a cigarette in front of two women; he was sitting on a wall facing the house and the two women."
- "He looked right at me. Someone yelled: 'Sheriff's Office.' I heard the faint pop of a taser gun. He immediately leaped forward and began to run toward the rear door of the residence."

<u>2. Second Deputy</u>

- "The sergeant said that when we arrive and see the suspect, if the suspect moves he and I are to use less lethal force with our tasers."

- "The sergeant said we are going to announce ourselves because he still has the weapon on him, we are going to taser him first if he moves at all."
- "We went through the fence door announcing ourselves 'Sheriff's Office, drop the gun, don't move.' The male subject stood up and the sergeant fired his taser."
- "At this time I heard 'Gun! Shoot!'"

3. Trainee Deputy Davis

- "A quick conversation took place between them at the location and afterwards he formulated us into an entry stack."
- "The sergeant peeked in through the gate and whispered to us that the male was in there sitting down with another male and female talking. We made entry."
- "I faced back and saw the suspect still in motion toward the house. I heard the scream of 'Gun! Shoot him!'"

The commonly-accepted police principle for situations like this and a raft of other incidents like robberies, burglaries, and hostage taking is succinctly summarized in "Contain, Control and Communicate." There was no time taken to assess the situation, no time expended in really planning an approach, no real effort to garner all the available background information, no containment of the area (all deputies entered at one point leaving the other sides of the backyard uncovered), additional deputies arriving almost simultaneously were not used to set up a perimeter, and no communication was attempted with the subject.

(Note: An indication of the precipitous entry is shown by the officers' reports indicating that there were "two" women in the back yard with Mr. Gordon. This is in contradiction to what they were told by Mr. Gordon's son that a male neighbor was talking with Mr. Gordon and his wife. The neighbor's long hair led the deputies to believe there were two women present.)

Conclusions

According to one deputy the sergeant made the decision to taser Mr. Gordon while they were walking up to the house i.e. "when we arrive…." Instructions coming from this supervisor were clear to the deputies that they were to taser and/or shoot if and when Mr. Gordon made any type of move. But it is apparent that Mr. Gordon was doing nothing at the time of their entry except sitting on the wall, smoking a cigarette, and talking with his wife and a neighbor.

The sudden and disruptive entry of the SWAT-type "stack" would have surprised anyone. It certainly surprised Mr. Gordon, who according to the deputy who fired the shots after the tasers went off, threw down the cigarette, stood up and lunged forward. Note the order of actions. He was tasered while he still had the cigarette in his mouth and their taser training indicates that the taser "shall not be used for subjects offering passive resistance behavior only." At the time that Mr. Gordon was tasered, he was offering no resistance, passive or active, to the deputies as he sat on the wall.

The use of force with the tasers was totally against the policy, the training, the requirements that subjects against which force is employed, be legitimately subject to arrest, be resistant, and threatening to the deputies.

A Proper Approach

An appropriate response would be as follows:

The call should have been considered as a "critical incident," with a proportionally extended police response, not merely of uniformed officers flooding the scene, but of specially trained and focused units assigned these comparatively more challenging tasks. The first responding deputies should have set up their perimeter and called in specialists.

But a situation where a suicidal person has a gun elevates the level of criticality. (Witness the combination of special resources called out for some suicidal persons in the Bethlehem (PA) Police Department policies.)

When a critical incident arises of this nature, a call should have gone out for extra personnel which could be SWAT (the department's equivalent of the ERT). This callout would also designate a Critical Incident Commander, a ranking person trained in handling the overall process of reining in the tendencies of SWAT to take action and simultaneously giving sufficient time to talk to the subject. (The SWAT commander should not be the Critical Incident Commander since the former has a greater orientation toward taking active steps and not giving time to the negotiator.)

In an ideal and ordered response, the responding deputies would have set up a perimeter around the yard. Possibly as more deputies arrived they would have gotten into the house itself. Most SWAT units are trained to handle all sorts of critical incidents and the possibility that in a suicide situation the subject might decide to take others' lives with his, would necessitate this trained unit. No attempt would have been made by the deputies to approach Mr. Gordon but deputies might have assured him that they were there to help, allowing one deputy to establish a little more personal relationship with him by being the only one to attempt communication from beyond the fence line.

A callout would have gone out for the departmental negotiator. Since it is confirmed that the department had a SWAT team it undoubtedly had a trained negotiator. The sergeant as a member of the SWAT unit would also be familiar with the capabilities of the negotiator from the eighty-five hours of SWAT training in his record. The negotiator's role would be to keep the dialogue going with hopes that Mr. Gordon would surrender the gun, and further referral might be made. A negotiator has all the time in the world to wait, to talk, to listen, to influence and to become a positive influence on the subject.

Police Administration by James Fyfe, Jack Greene, and William Walsh in the veritable bible for police managers in its 5th edition, 1997 states:

> "In response to this problem (the deinstitutionalization of Emotionally Disturbed Persons) training has been developed for police encounters with EDPs and generally encourages a patient, non-threatening approach in which officers keep their distance and demonstrate that they seek to help.
>
> "Unfortunately not all police have been adequately trained to deal with EDPs. As a result they sometimes apply to their encounters with EDPs the same techniques of deterrence through intimidation and threats of force that they have been trained to employ in their encounters with more rational offenders. These techniques often result in disaster."

Techniques which would force a knife-wielding robber to surrender, by pointing a gun at him, using a command voice and telling him there is no other viable option are effective, Fyfe remarks, but when:

> "police challenge a knife-wielding EDP in the same way or worse, close in on him to attempt to disarm him, those techniques are likely to precipitate attacks on themselves that can be halted only by resorting to deadly force."

He compares trying to intimidate an EDP into submission as no less likely to result in an explosion than is lighting the fuse to a stick of dynamite.

Shootings resorted to by police in dealing with EDPs where police attempt to intimidate them are unnecessary because they are caused by inappropriate and needlessly volatile police action, Fyfe states. His conclusion is clear:

> "Administrators should make certain that officers and all their colleagues on the line are adequately trained to deal with EDPs. It is tempting to place the blame for situations that have gone wrong at the level of execution, rather than to acknowledge policy or training deficiencies especially when doing so may expose a jurisdiction to liability for inadequate policy and training."

The barest of plans would have called for the sergeant's group to set up the perimeter, have one person attempt to talk with Mr. Gordon (since he was calmly talking with Jerri and Cartwright), appeared to be non-threatening while smoking and having a beer and chances were he would have resorted more positively. Immediate calls should have gone out for a negotiator and probably the SWAT team.

This was not done. There was no plan formulated with proper commitment to thinking the situation through, only a plan pre-determined, and not based on the specific incident but rashly devised by the sergeant while walking from the police cars to the house.

4. Was the use of deadly force against the subject objectively reasonable and justifiable?

The reckless and deliberate conduct during the attempted seizure of Mr. Gordon initially through the employment of the tasers along with the entire approach and surprise backyard invasion by the deputies in a SWAT-type entry was unreasonable, placing the deputies eventually in what they may have perceived, incorrectly, as a position of danger.

This incorrect perception could lead the deputies down the path to other actions (faulty or no planning, unreasonable utilization of the tasers, and unreasonably shooting Mr. Gordon) falling far short of police national standards, and eventually to the wrongful death of Mr. Gordon.

It bears repeating that even according to the statements of some of the deputies, Mr. Gordon was seated smoking a cigarette when the sudden "dynamic" entry of the deputies took place. As they rushed somewhat diagonally from the gate in the privacy fence in their "stack" toward the bend in the wall proximate to where Mr. Gordon was seated with the barest of announcements, the sergeant fired the first taser, and having missed directed the other deputy to fire a second.

Mr. Gordon in his current state, - depressed, sick of life, "pissed off," and having articulated suicidal thoughts, was startled by the flashlight shone in his face and immediately after by the taser dart landing in his arm. He responded quite naturally by standing up, and breaking for the door leading to the basement. The witnesses indicated he had nothing in his left hand at the moment of being aggressively attacked by the string of deputies.

The application of **Graham v. Connor** might be understandably blurred for members of the department since its "Use of Force" policy incorrectly highlights the principle of "subjective reasonableness" from **Johnson v. Glick** muddling the correct principles from **Graham** in their Use of Force policy.

Furthermore, **Johnson** again appears in the force training material presented for review and the principles from **Graham** are not mentioned or explained in their entirety. So with deficiencies in both policy and training documents the conditions for objective reasonableness were not adequately presented to the deputies for any use of force.

What was the government need or interest in invading the backyard, in firing tasers at Mr. Gordon, and then when as could be expected for a man in his condition, he moved toward his home? The extent and the quality of the intrusion totally outweigh the department's need for taking any action on a level with the ones they took.

As Mr. Gordon moved toward the house, there still was no offense which the group led by the sergeant could charge him with. Mr. Gordon posed no threat to any of the deputies by moving away from them. Certainly justification could not be based on the fact that he was a fleeing violent felon. There was no justifiable reason to arrest him, he was not actively resisting arrest, and he was startled by the abrupt entry of the "stack," the intrusion on his safety, and would naturally by the abrupt action of the team, as all the policy and training documents on dealing with the mentally ill state, react to force in such a manner.

In the chaotic scene engendered by the dynamic entry of the group, it is clearly documented in all three of the deputies' reports that someone said: "Gun! Shoot him!"

Since all three deputies heard the command, it was not issued by them; it could only have been issued by the sergeant, having realized that the ill-conceived plan to subdue and control Mr. Gordon with the tasers, while entirely unjustified and utterly objectively unreasonable, had failed.

The order was issued to the deputy who at the sergeant's direction had carried his rifle with him. This deputy fired three shots in a southerly direction while Mr. Gordon was moving toward the house. It is also apparent that Jerri, Mr. Gordon's wife, at the intrusion and the firing of the tasers, had moved backwards so that she was close to the same basement entry that Mr. Gordon was moving toward. Therefore, the deputy did not have a clear line of fire, and under the stress of the moment could have accidentally shot Jerri.

The deputy said he fired not because he was ordered to do so, but because he was threatened by Mr. Gordon's movements and so shot him in the back three times. But Mr. Gordon's position would not allow for an aggressive threat to the deputies who were behind him. The actions of this deputy constituted an unreasonable seizure of a man who could not be threatening him.

Reasonable officers in a similar situation would not have entertained such a foolish plan as the dynamic entry, the use of the tasers, and the use of deadly force. It was clearly objectively unreasonable for the deputy, even with the command, to fire his rifle three times into the back of a man moving away from him.

The totality of circumstances when considered do not allow this use of deadly force for it was a misguided situation from the start provoking an unstable man to react as he did because of the rash behavior of the sergeant's group which was far removed from any conformity to national standards for these types of incidents. Furthermore, the totality of circumstances when applied to the deputy's shooting of Mr. Gordon in the back falls far short of buttressing in any way his action.

An official record gave the arrival time on site as 23:02, three minutes and 16 seconds before the shots were fired. But allowing for the inconsistencies and the variations on the different communications records the twelve minute span between the first call and the shooting has to allow for response time for the four deputies, their conferring with Gordon's son, their approach to the backyard and their precipitous entry culminating in the attempted tasering of Mr. Gordon and his fatal shooting. The sergeant's team could only have been on the site for about three minutes before their unreasonable tactics and uses of force.

In the aftermath of Mr. Gordon's shooting, the sergeant directed the other three deputies to proceed to the front of the house and as the trainee deputy said: "To stand by at our vehicles and collect our thoughts," a clear violation of accepted standard procedures in the aftermath of an officer-involved shooting, to separate all those involved, not allowing the deputies to collect their thoughts together.

5. In the critical policy areas does the department follow its own policies?

There is probably no more critical area for review by the administration of any law enforcement agency than that conducted in the aftermath of an officer-involved shooting and of course in the more frequent usages of the upper levels of uses of force. Therefore in this case it is appropriate to scrutinize the department's policies relating to these two actions.

"Use of Force, Less Lethal, Electro-Muscular Disruption Device (EMDD)," states a report shall be filed:

> "Where the discharge was intentional and involved a use of force, a Use of Force report consistent with the requirements set forth in policies (Use of Force Documentation)."

It is the standard in law enforcement that when force is employed, it is not only the uses of force that actually strike a subject that are to be examined, but all uses of force whether they struck a subject or not. Why? To examine only the times when an officer fired his weapon and hit someone, would be for management not to be alerted to the important data that officers fire their weapons out of policy but fortunately do not hit the subject. All of the data on uses of force are important for management to be able to properly control the uses of force.

Therefore, for the use of the tasers, according to the policy we should find a Use of Force Report filed by the sergeant. It can be presumed that he did not file this report otherwise it would have been available for review. Additionally it must be noted that supervisors at various levels in the department did not recognize the violation of the policy.

As noted previously in the Use of Force policy:

> "All use of force must be documented in its entirety. The deputy will create a separate offense page. All supervisors in the chain of command will review the report. All other uses of force must be reported, i.e. OC, Striking, Kicking, Takedowns, Pain Compliance, Impact Weapons, and Firearms."

While tasers are not mentioned by name, they are by implication since Level 3 and Level 4 uses of force on the Use of Force Continuum are mentioned. Therefore, the policy was not followed; if it had been, then the department might have profited by the review and could have taken steps to guarantee that future employment of the tasers would not be directly against the policy.

Turning to the shooting investigation, it must be noted in the aftermath of this incident that the department directed its investigator, a lieutenant to Mirandize all four of their involved personnel. Once Mirandized, three of them chose not to make any statements; only the deputy who fired the shots did. However, all four wrote out statements under Garrity.

The actions taken by the lieutenant in management immediately after the incident are in clear violation of their own policies. Garrity and the administrative investigation by policy is to be performed by the Professional Standards Inspector and only when he determines that there is some possible violation of the law is his investigation terminated and a criminal investigation begun.

So, was it that the department management immediately felt there was a violation of the law and therefore Mirandized the deputies for according to their policy, once they did, they should have terminated the administrative investigation? Yet, having Mirandized the deputies, they continued what is obviously an administrative investigation.

Ultimately according to policy, the Professional Standards Inspector "will prepare a detailed report of findings for the sheriff, the Use of Force Review Board, and the County Attorney."

Be that as it may, the report prepared by the Professional Standards Inspector is to be presented to the sheriff, the Use of Deadly Force Review Board, and the County Attorney. This report presented to the Review Board will:

> "evaluate, in explicit and fact-finding fashion, each aspect of a deputy-involved shooting. Such evaluation will include:
>
> 1. a thorough review of the Shooting Incident Team's investigation report;
> 2. a thorough review of the Professional Standards report;
> 3. hearing of direct testimony, if necessary, from the deputy and witnesses."

The Review Board has the responsibility to develop its findings and recommendations in the following areas and present them to the sheriff as to:

> "1. Whether the shooting was within policy, or out of policy;
> 2. tactical considerations;
> 3. training considerations;

4. quality of supervision;
5. discipline considerations
6. the post incident investigative process and quality."

Finally the sheriff, after reviewing the Shooting Incident Team's investigation, and the report by Professional Standards and the findings of the Review Board, will ultimately determine whether the shooting was actually within the policy.

From documents submitted it appears that the report of the Professional Standards unit has been produced. This report has findings for both possible administrative and criminal violations. But there is no record of the Shooting Incident Team's Investigation, no record of the Use of Force Review Board's findings, and no indication of whether or not the sheriff eventually upheld the findings of Professional Standards even if two of the three investigations apparently were not performed.

By reason of his position, the sheriff is the policymaker and having written and issued the policies, he should be held responsible for not only the deputies' actions when they violate those policies, but he should also be held responsible when he does not follow his own policies. In this case he did not, and officially close to two years after the incident he has not ruled as to whether the shooting was within policy.

Actual conclusion of this case after two trials

Given the set of facts, it might surprise people to find that the federal court dropped everyone from the suit except the actual deputy who fired the three shots. The jury's verdict was he could have felt himself in danger of death or serious bodily injury; verdict for the defense.

APPENDIX B

<u>GALLAGHER'S RISK MANAGEMENT PRINCIPLES</u>

1. You can only beat or manage a system that you understand. Chiefs, sheriffs, supervisors and officers can beat any system that they understand.

If police really understand the methodologies of the liability process, and wanted to reduce its adverse impact, would we continue to adhere to the comparatively ineffective methods and practices that we do? An analysis of the liability process would readily surface the necessary methods to avoid its onerous burden.

For police there seems to be an incomplete understanding of the whole litigation process. It's not the test of beyond a reasonable doubt, but the preponderance of the evidence, an easier burden to achieve, that will determine the outcome. Evidence is presented in the form of depositions, documents and exhibits. Police would be familiar with direct and cross examination from their experience in criminal cases, but they are now the defendants, an unaccustomed role. There are organizational and personal consequences connected to their roles in the civil process and its subsequent outcome. An important component of the process is their policies, their training and a minute examination of their actions when picked apart by the plaintiffs' experts and attorneys.

2. The best process for managing police liability is quality supervision, good management and leadership with vision and values.

The burden of our efforts at avoiding liability must be proactive and active, ongoing quality supervision of all tasks with necessary corrections supported by observant and involved management guided by true leadership that is committed to a vision of a more highly effective and productive organization with high level performance supported and guided by values evidenced in all activities. Executives must see where they want to take the departments, to a place liberated from the onerous burden of much of the liability and strive to make their organizations "value-guided rather than policy-driven."

3. To win in the liability game you have to understand and think like the opposition.

The qualities that characterize great officers and investigators must be applied to the problem of liability. Surveillance must be constant to see what is transpiring; evidence must be gathered and analyzed; finally appropriate steps must be taken. But this focus must be centered on what the opposition does and how it does it. Understand how the opposition thrives on alleged poor performance, and how they craft their interpretation of the facts into a complaint and eventually a full blown lawsuit. Counter their search for opportunities to sue police by denying them their basic resource, incidents falling short of standards. Understanding their objectives can only drive police to implement steps denying the plaintiffs' bar the chance to file actions. If police truly understand how the opposition operates the reactions should be automatic. If we don't truly understand, then we are onerously burdening ourselves and our organizations. If we understand and do nothing, then we only have ourselves to blame. There is incalculable value in this concentration if it successfully leads us to change certain patterns in our thinking and performance.

4. The plaintiff's game plan is an open book. Read it and act accordingly.

The plaintiff and his attorney can only initiate an action, a lawsuit if they can generate questions about the manner in which officers performed their tasks. If police refuse to grant them any leverage upon which to start an action by their performance, then the opening is denied the plaintiffs and plans for litigation are thwarted. Police know explicitly their game plan. With that in mind, it should be easy to deny them an opportunity to move against us.

5. Liability is a good force if we learn how to use it to further our goals, which should be higher professional standards. As a lever liability if used properly can change the system.

The policing profession has been improved because we have been forced to change as a result of lawsuits. Those changes have been effected slowly because maybe the messages from the lawsuits have been somewhat muted, not totally heard, and at times ignored even when repeated in various ways in case law. But there is little excuse not to hear clearly and immediately the message of the courts and to respond accordingly. Change through the process of litigation and the resultant judgments and decisions will be facilitated if only we listen and act. But in this manner the profession is reacting; it would be easier if it were more proactive and were to get out in front of the issues, amend policy, develop training, and offer the example of a profession providing its own direction rather than having it forced upon it.

6. Policy is to be developed and issued in anticipation of the foreseeable field incidents that officers can reasonably be expected to encounter. Policy that is subsequent and in reaction to a series of events encountered by officers is more likely to be deficient and is issued in the face of a growing organizational pattern of conduct contrary to the substance of the policy.

It must be seen it is the obligation of the policymaker, i.e. the chief of police to provide administrative guidance to the officers in anticipation of the assigned tasks. In reality the officers have a right to these directives not necessarily to take away their discretion but to channel it, to guide them as to how they are to perform the tasks assigned to them. When policies are not written proactively, when there is little or no training in the requirements of the policies, then the policymaker can rest assured that certain patterns of conduct will become the custom and practice in the absence of the necessary guidance. Once embedded in practice, it will be much harder to institute the correct practices when it is then deemed obligatory.

Policy must be proactive, not reactive. Policymakers must provide administrative guidance on all the tasks to be performed by their officers.

Policy must be reinforced by training from the academy and through in-service and through the accountability of supervisors who judiciously require some remediation or retraining when necessary.

7. There is no factor more important to the avoidance of liability and the upgrading of the agency's professional performance and attainment of its standards than the quality of supervision.

There are many demands on supervisors. Improvement in our position against liability means even more demands and concurrently more support and accountability from the second level of supervision. The mantle of supervision must be accorded those who are comprehensively trained and tightly supervised themselves.

8. Discipline in its reactive mode is in essence a failure on the part of the proactive components: policy, training, and supervision to achieve the desired results and might develop from the absence of performance planning. Discipline and remediation, at once fair and progressive, is an indication that the supervisory function is truly active and functioning.

To change performance it must be recognized that there are three phases: proactive, that is policies and training; active, supervision; and reactive, discipline, inspections and evaluations. In an ideal environment the proactive and active phases should engender high level performance. When parts of those are ineffective or not properly embedded in the organization, discipline and corrective action are necessary. Our efforts should be to so improve the first two phases so that discipline is not needed but when introduced it respects the individual, is evenly administered and is progressive to the extent that in some cases it must end in termination.

9. If we don't want to pay the price of doing business the way we are, then we have to change the way we do business. If we don't mind paying the price, then we shouldn't change the way we do business.

Amid all the criticism of plaintiffs' lawyers and their clients, about the awards given to them either in settlements or in judgments by juries, I feel that the profession has dulled its attention to the available methods of reducing the initiation of lawsuits. In sounding off against the costs of liability, we must realize that reducing the costs requires the profession to make some appropriate but not necessarily radical changes to the manner in which leadership, management and supervision are provided. Certainly performance must be targeted through every means available. We have to change; the sooner the better. If we do not change then we will implicitly accept the fiscal and organizational burden of liability.

10. In risk management, the best defense is a good offense. Winning is a lot more fun than losing.

This means an active commitment to a proactive stance one that yields no ground to the opposition. This plan deprives them of their critical resource: low level performance, potential negligent actions or supposed constitutional violations. It places the highest emphasis on optimum performance, and when it is not attained, it takes appropriate steps to assure it continues in the future. If followed religiously, then there is only a decreasing number of incidents that have to be defended. Win at the earliest possible point. Front end load the process for success

11. Deny the plaintiff's attorney access to the departmental management's major defense points: policies, training, and supervision. You will have appreciably reduced the chances of losses and/or the size of the losses.

This denial of access to these points allows the defense to concentrate on the officer. Too often concern about deficient policies and training or the inadequate involvement of supervisors in the incident encourages the move toward some form of settlement. If those factors are solidly in place, then they should support the actions of the officer.

12. Issuing policy is easy. The most difficult challenge, met through training, supervision, and performance management, is getting people to follow the policy.

The profession has turned out countless reams of policies; manuals in many cases are inches thick. What effect have they had on performance? How much do they really control the actions of officers? How effectively has our training and supervision supported policies? Have we let too many examples of performance out of policy go unnoticed? Uncorrected? If policy is truly worthwhile, then it must be reinforced constantly by training and supervision otherwise it loses most of its effectiveness to forge higher levels of performance. In that case it usually becomes involved after the fact, for something has gone wrong and we search the manuals to find out exactly how the conduct was short of the standards. That is not the method for having policy become effective; it is not the method for diminishing liability.

13. Increasingly in the post-<u>Canton</u> era, police training will be attacked and found inadequate.

We have yet to see the scrutiny of police training that in my opinion will certainly transpire in the immediate future. I feel that plaintiffs' attorneys, when they include as part of their complaints a charge of negligent training, have not come anywhere close to mining the deficiencies in actual training and testing for competence in that subject. The bar for reaching the standard enunciated in **Canton** will be raised in the sense that more forceful and better articulated attacks will be established on all levels of training. In the main, no profession can offer sustained high level performance without constantly increasing the quantity and quality of training.

14. The attacks on police training will feature more emphasis on the adequacy of police training from a substantive and a methodological basis.

Given the multiplicity of tasks that an officer has to perform and perform well, we must realize that training has to be lengthened and improved. Decision making has to be integrated into the acquisition of knowledge and skills. Problem-based training must be incorporated into as many aspects of training as possible. The lecture technique must be seen as inadequate to prepare officers for the application of their training to the actual incidents they will face on the streets. States must develop a type of police officer competency examination, something akin to a Bar exam, to raise the standards in all training centers and to ensure that officers are better prepared to at least a minimum level of proficiency. Passage of this examination will allow the officer to be sworn in. In certain areas essay questions must be presented to better assess an officer's comprehension of subject matter.

15. A direct correlation exists between good management and quality supervision and the management of liability.

It is obvious that risk management for the most part demands a similar type of competence that must exist in any efficient and effective managerial and supervisory environment. Our failure at improving management, supervision and accountability constitutes the grounds for our failing to curb liability.

16. Police departments must worship at the altar of high level performance. They must remember that policies, training, supervision, and discipline are merely inputs to achieve that. The only acceptable output is high level performance. That is the only thing that the public expects and has a right to.

While the constant improvement in policies, training, and supervision is commendable and necessary that must not be seen as anything close to the required improvement. It is only when that improvement affects performance and better quality of every level of service that we have the truly desired output. We should not confuse inputs into the system with the hoped for output, the only one that is accepted and desirable, the only one that truly justifies the existence of the agency. That is high level performance.

Too often in confusing inputs with the required outputs, police can become complacent for they have totally revised the policy manual, they have established new levels of basic and in-service training, they have achieved a lower supervisor- to-officer ratio. Those are truly advances, and it is hoped that good things will come, that performance will be raised. While these inputs can be quite tangible what must be measured and weighed is the impact on performance. The inputs do not touch people's lives; it is the output in the quality of performance and service that does.

17. Most catastrophic judgments result from ignoring the fundamentals over which we have control as chiefs, managers, and supervisors.

The salient point is that in the work of policing it is the small things that matter. When there is not the rigid attention to details there enters the potential for a possible major problem. Police cannot control all the actions that people take in confrontational situations. But they can to a high degree of certainty guarantee through direction, training and supervision that the professional standards associated with these tasks are present in every encounter. There is a tendency when the outcome of an incident is successful, e.g. the person is controlled, the subject is pulled over after a pursuit that supervisors tend to overlook any breaches of policies or training. However, over time, the shortcomings in performance may reoccur to haunt us when something does go wrong, something is not done properly and the result is regrettable.

18. Performance is elevated proactively by policy, training and values; actively by supervision, and reactively by audits, evaluations, discipline, reports, inspections, remediation, and commendations.

To elevate performance it must be understood there is a continuum of influences essential to achieve that outcome. Performance is affected before the person does something in preparation for that activity. It is then influenced in a daily manner by the active oversight and guidance of supervision. Finally after the person has done the tasks, performance must be reviewed, evaluated, corrected, and commended if appropriate. The optimal efforts in one phase, such as the proactive phase, will not make up for the absence of active and reactive influences for performance is elevated by what takes place before persons act, while persons are acting, and finally by what is done after they act. If the process is deficient or truncated, then we cannot expect anything close to the desired results.

19. The focus of every complaint, claim, or lawsuit is an allegation police performance was short of professional standards.

What must become clear to us is that these formal demands made on police departments have as their central theme, the quality of the performance that the person received. It is alleged these persons are not satisfied, that the service provided to them was negligent, or that there was some violation of constitutional rights. To diminish the liability burden, police have to decrease these demands by raising the performance standards of every action they take. Nothing else matters.

20. Anything that inhibits high level performance must be decreased or eliminated; anything that helps officers perform better must be increased.

Within any organization efforts must be made to detect those factors that affect performance negatively, and then they must be eliminated to the extent possible. On the other hand, supervisors must realize that they are there to help people perform better, so whatever raises the level of performance, whatever makes them better officers, should be emphasized.

21. Critique to learn, not to blame.

Organizations can achieve greater success if the supervisory and managerial climate is conducive to the growth of individuals, especially if they can learn from any mistakes made. Too often when anything untoward happens, there is a rush to assign blame resulting in a culture opposed to its members' personal and professional growth. On the contrary, if any reviews or critiques occur in an atmosphere where the goal is to learn from the incident there is more of a chance of people getting better, and the relationship between different levels in the organization is improved. There are invaluable lessons that should be extracted from a critical review but to garner the most attention must be paid to the manner in which it is carried out and the manner in which persons are addressed.

22. Policy is only as effective as the training in the substance and requirements of that policy. If training is weak, unfocused or non-existent, then the policy will not be followed. Training must also cover the full range of the High Risk/Critical Tasks which officers are expected to perform.

If the policies are as important as it would seem from their critical role in attempting to raise performance to the highest levels, you would think that a necessary corollary would be that from the start of basic training officers-to-be would be schooled in their requirements. You would also think that all officers would know the contents of new and revised policies and that policies would be featured in all in-service training. If this is not done for all policies, then certainly for the High Risk/Critical Task policies. This is not the case. The role of policies for all their imputed importance is downgraded by the failure to form the complete process for achieving the desired results, i.e. training and essential application to operations. The policy process is truncated after the issuance of policies. For all the energy and resources given to the development and improvement of police policies, the profession garners only a modicum of benefit. Policies play a more prominent role after the fact, in reviewing police actions, when they are held up to see if the officers followed the policies or violated them.

23. **Policies are not learned by placing them in an officer's mailbox (virtual or actual), nor learned by telling officers to "read and understand" the manual, and not learned and made operational by having sergeants comment on them at roll calls.**

If ten sergeants were tasked with commenting on a new policy, what is the guarantee that the commentary would have any semblance of uniformity? Yes, not all incidents are the same, but through constant application of the policies to scenarios and in reviews of actual incidents minimally a greater understanding will develop over the expected requirements of the policy.

Generally the police profession has come a considerable distance from the days when copies of policies were placed in officers' mailboxes, where newly minted officers were given a thick looseleaf binder of all the policies and directives and simultaneously were required to sign a form that they had "read and understood" all the policies. The technology exists to have all policies forwarded via email to all officers who then acknowledge their receipt. But there is still little actual training on the content and application of the policies themselves. Would that the transmission of the policy contents were to be accompanied by a series of questions related to scenarios.

24. **The challenge to win the liability struggle begins on the street; it is not only won in court.**

The more the police profession becomes less reactive and more proactive about dealing with liability, the more effective it will be. All of our strategies must be directed towards the point in time where the action takes place, the street. Directing our efforts there will have the biggest payoffs in the form of reduced lawsuits, because the performance of our officers is at such a level as to give no reason or cause for any action to be filed for negligence or possible constitutional violations. It is the means to starve plaintiffs' attorneys rather than feed them a rich diet of potential litigation.

25. Police gather data on performance and plaintiffs' attorneys analyze them.

While police departments accumulate a lot of data through the filing of incident and follow-up reports, through investigatory files, and anything related to performance data, there is little systemic review and analysis of them. Despite the need for management to base critical decisions on data, this is not usually accomplished. Plaintiffs' attorneys in their requests for production of documents (even if they have to make repeated requests) can get their hands on a good deal of the data. Once they receive this, their analysis may expose the failure of management to track on patterns of conduct or even problem officers. The timely analysis by police of all data related to operations and officer conduct allows them to make necessary changes.

26. There is nothing you should do to manage liability that you should not already be doing as a good leader, good manager, a good supervisor, and a good officer.

Finally there is no real secret to managing liability other than striving to fulfill your job description as perfectly as possible. By improving your performance you will directly and even indirectly improve others' performance. Simultaneously the liability problem will erode. It can be said the problem with liability has grown because of the shortcomings in our managerial and supervisory performance, and our failure to uphold professional standards permeated with the stated values of our organization.

ABOUT THE AUTHOR

G. Patrick Gallagher, president of the Gallagher-Westfall Group, is a nationally recognized expert in law enforcement liability. <u>**Successful Police Risk Management**</u> follows his 1992 book on the same topic: <u>**Risk Management behind the Blue Curtain**</u>. In addition to conducting hundreds of training sessions focusing on high risk/critical tasks such as pursuit and uses of force for police supervisors, managers and chiefs of police in all 50 states, he has conducted risk assessments, audits, investigations, and management reviews for law enforcement agencies focusing on evaluations of their operations, policies and procedures, management and leadership styles, organizational climate and generally any factor that might contribute to the presence of potential or actual liability in those organizations. Gallagher's training programs have also focused on leadership development, management and supervisory responsibilities and policy development. Furthermore as an expert witness, his involvement has focused on all levels of use of force, the emergency operations of police vehicles and arrests.

Previously Gallagher was appointed Director of Criminal Justice Standards and Training for the state of Florida by then Governor Bob Graham in 1980 where he administered the policies established by the Criminal Justice Standards and Training Commission and was responsible for enforcing standards of employment, training and certification requirements for all of the state's police and corrections officers. Furthermore he enforced standards for all training centers, all curricula, and all instructors while also dealing with the decertification of officers who did not maintain original standards. In other positions, Gallagher was Director of the Police Executive Institute at the Police Foundation in D.C. providing executive development programs to the country's largest law enforcement agencies. Finally he was also Director of Public Safety in South Bend (IN) for the police and fire departments.

Gallagher has also co-authored with Dr. Ian McKenzie, Chief Superintendent, London Metropolitan Police (ret.) **Behind the Uniform**, a study of comparative policing. He has been a columnist for the British Police Review, has authored numerous articles dealing with police liability, and has produced a syndicated column on police liability in the U.S. He has been a member of the International Association of Chiefs of Police, the Police Executive Research Forum, the National Association of Internal Affairs Investigators, the American Society of Law Enforcement Training, the Public Risk Management Association, and the International Association of Directors of Law Enforcement Standards and Training. Gallagher received his BA from Marist College, his MA from New York University, and completed his Ph.D. course work at Purdue University.

**Gallagher-Westfall Group P.O. Box 310   Springtown, PA. 18081
Ph: 610/346/6637   www.gallagherpoliceexpert.com**

TRAINING AVAILABLE

For those interested in having **G. Patrick Gallagher** share his ideas on police risk management presented in this book with groups of police managers and executives, for the directors and managers of risk management and insurance pools, for police defense attorneys, and for local officials, all concerned about the burden that police liability is having on law enforcement, he will customize programs of various lengths. So for annual conferences or meetings or regular training sessions he will schedule programs to fit your needs.

Please contact him at:

gpatrickgallagher11@verizon.net or call at: 610/346/6637